12th Century Coffin Lid at St Peter's Church Northampton

NORTHAMPTONSHIRE TREASURES

a personal selection by Ernest Reynolds

published by Ruth Bean, Emberton, Olney, Buckinghamshire in 1972

Design by Paul Torr
Typeset in 11pt Baskerville
Published by Ruth Bean, Emberton, Olney, Buckinghamshire

Printed in Great Britain by
Scolar Press Limited, Menston, Yorkshire

Foreword

Most of the essays contained in this book are reprinted by courtesy of the Northampton Independent Ltd., publishers of "The Northampton and County Independent", to whom grateful acknowledgement is made.

"Taverns of the Town", "Queen Eleanor's Cross", "The Northampton Churches of Matthew Holding", "Northampton Market Square" and articles on Northampton Town Hall and Repertory Theatre from which extracts have been taken, originally appeared in the magazine "Town Affairs" and are reprinted by kind permission of the publishers, The Belmont Press, Northampton.

Without the generous assistance of many individuals and organisations of Northamptonshire this book would never have appeared. In particular we would like to thank the staff of the Northampton Public Library, especially Mr John Stafford the Local History Librarian, for their constant help and encouragement. We are very grateful to the Library, to the Northampton Development Corporation and Central Art Gallery and Museum, to Mrs Daisy Mace, Mr Bruce Bailey, Sir Gyles Isham and Mr T. Osborne Robinson, as well as to many other kind persons who have helped in various ways with the illustrations, providing loans of material, research and permission for reproduction.

We hope the result will bring pleasure to many people.

The great majority of the places and works of art described here are fully accessible to the public, but several of the private mansions, such as Easton Neston, Boughton House and Lamport Hall, are not normally open at all, though sometimes the gardens may be shown in Summer for charitable purposes.

Althorp, Burghley and Castle Ashby, however, can always be visited at certain advertised times, and it is advisable to check on these before planning any detailed itinerary.

A useful guide, published annually by ABC Travel Guides Ltd., Dunstable, Bedfordshire at 30p is "Historic Houses, Castles & Gardens in Great Britain and Ireland". This gives individual opening times and amenities.

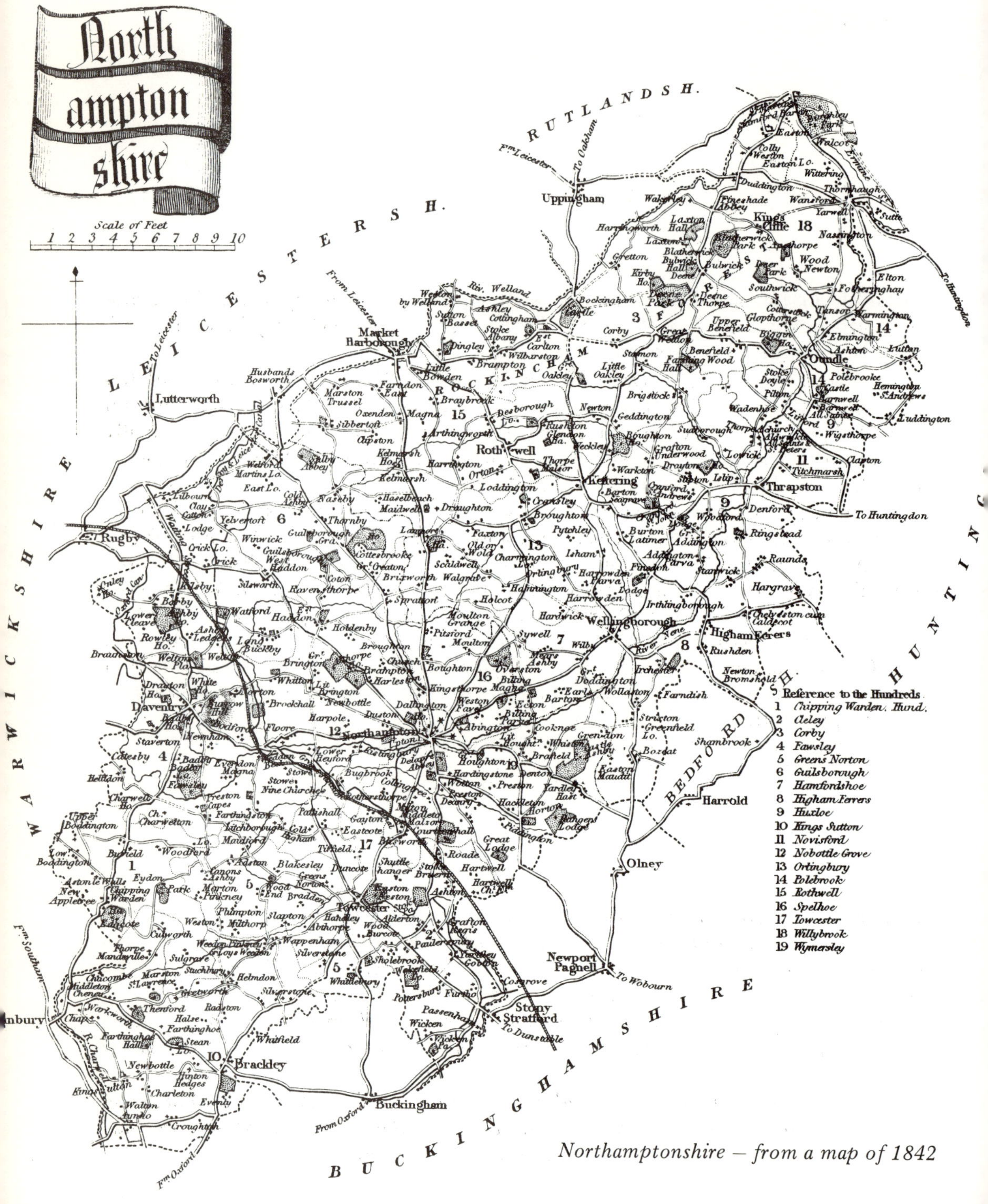

Northamptonshire – from a map of 1842

Contents

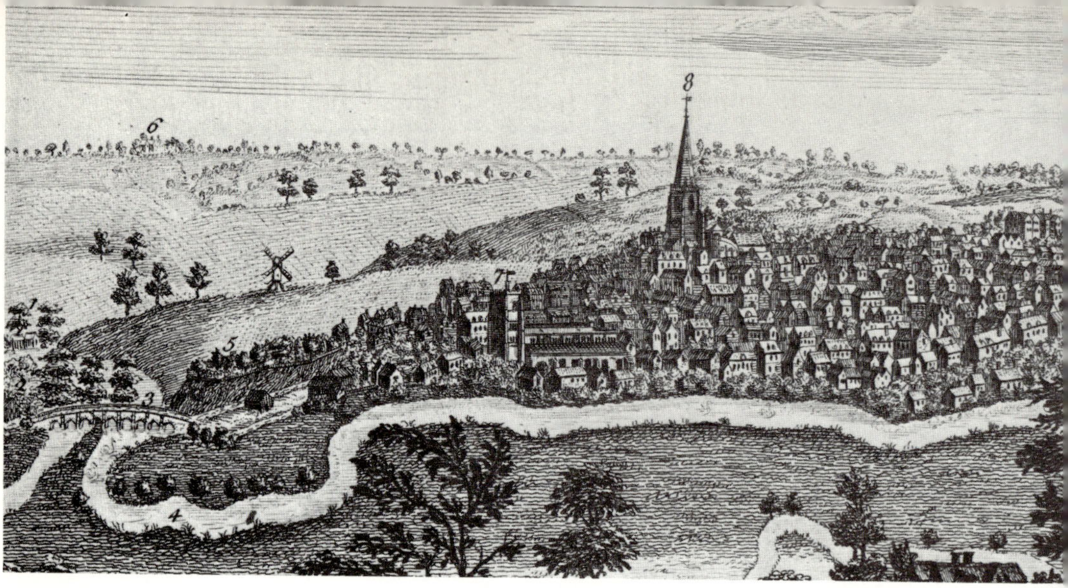

Introduction

At the end of 1968 the Editor of "The Northampton and County Independent", Mr. Lou Warwick, asked me if I would write a series of articles about Northamptonshire to be entitled "County Treasures", leaving the selection of subjects entirely to me.

I was very glad to do this, principally because it is always pleasant to be given a free hand in the choice of material and to feel that there is no specified ground to cover as in the ordinary guidebook type of descriptive writing.

Originally I thought of selecting only from the rich store of fine historical buildings of Northamptonshire, but one or two other treasures, such as the magnificent Spanish cabinet which had been recently acquired by the Northampton Central Museum, the baroque organ at Towcester and the beautiful Morris stained glass windows at Middleton Cheney, somehow crept into the series. Also two splendid paintings, one now a permanent Northampton treasure and another which was on loan from Sir Gyles Isham's home at Lamport Hall.

This book is mainly a reprint of that "Independent" series, which ran from January 1969 to December 1970, together with one or two essays about Northampton town which I wrote for the magazine "Town Affairs". There is also one which appeared in the "Independent", but separately from the original series, on the exquisitely beautiful little Victorian Theatre Royal and Opera House at Northampton which has been for so long the home of the Northampton Repertory Company.

Finally there are two completely new essays, one on the ancient churches of Northampton and one on Earl Spencer's famous house at Althorp Park.

Mr. Warwick not only left the selection of topics to me but let me vary the style as I chose from occasional personal reminiscence to more detailed description, and I have kept these varieties of style in the present collection.

South West Prospect of Northampton, 18th Century.
Numbers 7, 8, 9 and 12 are the four ancient churches of Northampton — see p.49.

Anyone seeking a full gazetteer of everything of architectural note in Northamptonshire will naturally turn to Sir Nikolaus Pevsner's "Northamptonshire" in "The Buildings of England" series, a work which is admirably detailed, learned, readable, and backed by the judgement of one of the most distinguished architectural writers in Europe. And there are several other good guidebooks on the county available for those who want to plan a complete itinerary.

A glance at the contents of this book, however, will show at once that it is not intended to compete with these. It is not offered as a comprehensive guide to the hundreds of treasures in Northamptonshire but simply as a personal selection which I hope will encourage many visitors and travellers to explore further for themselves what our fascinating county has to offer.

The full list of major places of interest in Northamptonshire includes many more than I have mentioned here and ranges from world-famous churches, such as the seventh century basilican fabric at Brixworth and the stately procession of masterpieces down the Nene Valley, to fantastic conceits such as Sir Thomas Tresham's Triangular Lodge at Rushton Hall and Victorian splendours like Sir Gilbert Scott's rich chancel at Ashley.

There are, too, more recent masterpieces such as Sir Ninian Comper's St. Mary's at Wellingborough which is one of the great sights of the county, a glorious riot of blue and gold, with a sumptuous baldachino, rich fittings and an exterior in lovely golden ironstone.

In fact, wherever you travel in Northamptonshire you will find something of absorbing interest; a splendid spire, like King's Sutton in the south west of the county, great country houses such as Drayton and the splendid ruin of Kirby Hall, charming village cottages with highpitched roofs and places with famous memories like Naseby and Delapre Park where the Battle of Northampton was fought in 1460.

Our Undiscovered Treasures

It is surprising how many people, during the summer months, neglect the treasures of Northamptonshire in favour of excursions further afield.

From May onwards our roads become crowded with cars speeding either through or out of Northamptonshire, but not nearly enough motorists pause to explore the beauties virtually on their own doorstep. Perhaps this is in some ways a good thing since, while Evesham and Broadway and Stratford-on-Avon are chockablock with vehicles, the beauties of Northamptonshire remain delightfully uncluttered.

But on their own merit many of our lovely sights are worthy of far more attention than they receive. How many counties, for instance, can show such a marvel as Burghley House, that "astonishing apparition" as it has been called, only an hour or so from the county town itself? With its Black and Yellow Bedchamber, its Green Damask Room, its glittering array of masterpieces by Veronese, Rembrandt and Gainsborough, its superb "Heaven Room" by Verrio, generally considered the finest painted room in England, the fabulous Queen Anne silver cistern, the largest in the world, and the sumptuous surroundings including the Chinese Orange Court, Burghley is worth a whole day's journey, let alone a few short miles. Other treasures of the house include a jewel casket in silver, tortoiseshell and malachite, presented by the unfortunate Nicholas II, the last Czar of Russia, masterpieces of Georgian silver, marble and porphyry, a Pagoda Room with a model Nankin pagoda, a bed with coral and white satin hangings, and some magnificent Soho tapestries in Queen Elizabeth's bedroom.

Even so close and famous a local wonder as Castle Ashby is still a pleasure in store for many Northamptonshire people. And what a splendid ensemble it makes, with its balustraded gardens, its delightful church and its treasure-chest of wonders within. The porcelain and the pictures, including the famous Mantegna, are alone worth a visit. But the carved staircase, the panelled chapel, the tapestries and fine furniture and the Inigo Jones gallery are all enchanting treasures to be enjoyed, not once but on many visits, year in and year out. "The Connoisseur" has frequently featured some of the exquisite furnishings of Althorp House; this splendid mansion, with its unrivalled picture gallery of masterpieces, is also within a few minutes of Northampton, and makes a fine short excursion for a summer afternoon.

A very good base for exploration in Northamptonshire is Kettering which gives rapid access to a host of interesting places, famous and (often equally fascinating) not so well known. I am constantly discovering fresh delights in this part of Northamptonshire, such as the splendid Victorian church at Orlingbury, built by Hussey in the 1840's. And there are lovely villages like Weekley, with its nearby French chateau style mansion, and Warkton with its marvellous 18th century sculpture in the church chancel. Rothwell, a charming little town with Northamptonshire's longest church that

Carved Staircase, Castle Ashby (copyright Country Life)

has a handsome tawny golden stone interior, is another somewhat neglected gem in the local diadem.

But for my own part I am never so happy as when browsing among the lesser known Edwardian buildings of the county, neglected as they are by all but a few devotees. And Northamptonshire, along with many fine Edwardian houses, has one of the most glorious of all Edwardian churches in the whole of England, yet many local people never seem to have heard of it. I mean, of course, that magnificent masterpiece by Sir Ninian Comper, St. Mary's at Wellingborough, which I return to again and again for mental refreshment, and delight whenever I am in its vicinity.

St Mary's Church, Wellingborough

Do you know St. Mary's? Set away from the town centre, right down against the railway station and surrounded by late Victorian and Edwardian streets, it is a miracle in golden-brown stone with a dazzling and glorious interior in blue and gold, though still, alas, unfinished in all its glittering detail.

If St. Mary's were in Austria or Italy or France it would be flocked to as a great tourist sight. But because it is only in Wellingborough thousands of people who could easily visit it never do so. Magnificent enough even now, with its superb vistas of fan-vaulting and glistening organ-case and golden baldachino, it will one day be still more sumptuous. And when it is finished Northamptonshire will then have one of the finest twentieth century buildings in the whole of England.

St. Mary's particularly fascinates me for it is part of that wonderful legacy of Victorian and Edwardian architecture which has suffered so much from spoiling and demolition during the last dozen years or so. The more people visit buildings like St. Mary's the more I believe they will come to realise what a splendid heritage our immediate ancestors left us and how infinitely well worth preserving its best specimens are.

Northamptonshire has lots of unsuspected pleasures of this kind to offer. So it is well worth remembering that not by any means all the finest sights of English civilisation date from long ago. Many of them, like St. Mary's, were put up by the generation of our own fathers and grandfathers, and they can be richly rewarding to those with a sympathetic eye.

Northampton Town Hall

Right in the heart of Northampton stands one of our principal County Treasures, the magnificent Victorian Gothic Town Hall. Open almost any history of English architecture from Queen Victoria onwards and you will find mention of this splendid masterpiece by Godwin and Northampton's own brilliant architect, Matthew Holding.

Now that the reaction against Victorian architecture has almost completely passed away, this fine Town Hall is being more and more admired. In actual fact it is an extremely rich architectural conception, and if only its facade were better placed, say in the Market Square where it could be properly seen, it would be even more famous among the connoisseurs of Victoriana than it already is. With a touch of that Venetian Gothic so beloved of Ruskin, and a flavouring of the flamboyance of a French mediaeval cathedral, the building is yet essentially English in its composition. Illuminated clock-tower, arched and vaulted Council Chamber and serried rows of beautifully sculptured windows combine to produce an effect of solemn and yet comfortable-looking grandeur which is well in keeping with our national tradition.

Theatrical, in a sense, the design certainly is, since most of the resources of the architects were lavished on the magnificent facade, leaving the back (and even some of the interior) to take care of itself, though no lover of the Gothic Revival could fail to admire the excellence of the Council

Northampton Town Hall at the turn of the Century

Chamber and the polychromatic arabesques of the first-floor corridor and its double staircase.

The actual building material was good in itself, with its alternating grey and yellow-brown, though time has somewhat blackened the grey and dulled the brown. Even so, one cannot help wishing that the builders had chosen that glorious golden-coloured Northamptonshire stone which is one of the most beautiful materials in the world and which gives such a comforting perfection to so many of our village houses and county churches. But seen in rainy sunlight, or faintly silvering morning mist, or on a blue and golden October afternoon, the general effect of the stonework is beautiful enough.

Northampton was remarkably well served by the Victorians and you have only to look at, say St. Matthew's Church, the highly skilled additions to St. Sepulchre's Church, the old Opera House (now the Repertory Theatre) and many of the town's fine private houses, to see the truth of this.

But of everything Victorian the town possesses, the Town Hall is easily the finest gem. Its rich sculptural facade is a kind of stone history book of Northamptonshire. Statues ranging from St. Thomas a Becket to Queen Victoria adorn the long frontage and include Richard I, Edward IV, Queen Eleanor, Dryden and even St. Patrick, who, according to some writers, was born in Northamptonshire.

It is a common criticism of Victorian civic and ecclesiastical architecture that its sculpture was poor, its figures lifeless, and its decorative detail badly executed. This unfortunately, was often true, and the facade of Lichfield Cathedral might be cited in support, for when the nineteenth century restorers had done their worst with the array of saints on Lichfield's West Front, the effect was jejune and flat in the extreme. But the carved scenes from Northampton's history over our Town Hall windows need fear no criticism of this kind. Each was

Statue of St Patrick

a fresh conception, freshly imagined and designed and just as freshly executed. The scenes represent (right to left): Edward I giving orders for the erection of the Eleanor Cross at Northampton; Henry VI bestowing on the town a charter; Henry II doing the same; the wedding of Waltheof and Judith, niece of William the Conqueror; the Fire of Northampton, 1675; the Battle of Naseby 1645; the execution of Mary Queen of Scots; the foundation of Northampton Grammar School; Edward IV meeting Elizabeth Woodville at Grafton Regis; and the Trial of St. Thomas a Becket at Northampton Castle. And there is a wealth of interesting subsidiary detail, such as a series of Aesop's Fables, over fifty heraldic shields, with those of Higham Ferrers, Daventry, Brackley, Lawrence Washington of Sulgrave, Peterborough and dozens more.

Another exquisite feature of the exterior is the lovely lead spire or fleche, which, though easy to overlook from St. Giles's Square, is a piece of craftsmanship worthy of comparison with the spirelet of Exeter College, Oxford.

The interior has panels by a distinguished artist, Colin Gill, with Alfred the Great, Charles I, Cromwell, and Northampton's most famous M.P., Spencer Perceval, who was assassinated in the House of Commons while he was actually Prime Minister.

The whole of this magnificent building, together with the masterly extension made by Matthew Holding and A. W. Jeffery in 1892, cost Northampton only £67,620 2s. 1d. Today, even assuming that such a structure were a possible architectural proposition it would cost a million pounds at the very least, and almost certainly more.

I am glad to learn that it has recently acquired a Ghost, though who the restless figure may be is a matter of conjecture. The Ghost of Godwin, I should imagine, come to haunt any Town Council which might maltreat his handsome work. A particular feature in the building's recent history has been the erecting of the Venetian-style flag-staffs and lamps outside, now painted an attractive red.

Town Hall and All Saints' Church

Panelled Oak Room at Abington Park Museum

The Curious Case of the Missing Coffins

Three hundred years ago Lady Elizabeth Barnard, Shakespeare's grand-daughter and his last descendant, died at Abington Manor, now the Abington Park Museum of Northampton. She was 64. The mystery of Shakespeare's missing manuscripts, which she presumably inherited along with the rest of the poet's estate, has never been solved, and probably it never will. For many years there was a lively legend that the precious papers were concealed somewhere in the present Museum, with the panelling of the famous Oak Room as a probable hiding hole.

This fable is now generally discredited though in fact the panelling has never been completely dismantled to investigate. But the Manor was finally sold by Lady Elizabeth's husband to the Thursby family and they largely rebuilt it around 1740 when any valuable relics would surely have come to light. The Thursbys were, besides, interested in Shakespeare, and Garrick, the most famous Shakespearean actor of the eighteenth century, actually stayed at the house as their guest.

Also, a general search of the house was made some years back to see if anything could be discovered, but nothing whatever was found.

But the whole business begins to take on a touch of Sherlock Holmes with the curious affair of Lady Elizabeth's grave. She definitely died at Abington Manor and the entry of her burial can still be seen in the Abington Parish Register for February, 1669. It is presumed that she must have been buried in the same grave as her husband (in the south aisle of the church), but there was no inscription recording this until fairly recently when a brief statement about her was cut on the flagstone tomb. And both the coffins of Sir John and of Lady Elizabeth seem to have vanished without trace.

Did someone anticipate a rich reward from the opening of the tomb? Could the coffin of Lady Elizabeth have been known to contain valuable mementoes of her famous grandfather? Has the coffin been removed to some nearby place, either in the churchyard or somewhere in the park or its vicinity? Are the precious papers, in fact, mysteriously somewhere at Abington still? Did the theft from the tomb take place when the church's plate was stolen in 1807?

We can probably rule out the possibility of any manuscripts of the actual plays of Shakespeare having ever been at Abington at all. They would far more likely have been retained in London after the poet's death, either at the Globe Theatre (they would have been the theatre's property) or at the office of the printers of the First Folio, which appeared in 1623. And if so they may well have perished in one of the many fires of the seventeenth century, perhaps the Great Fire of London in 1666. But Shakespeare wrote much poetry other than the plays, and Elizabeth would surely have inherited some specimens of this. And if so she would have brought them with her when she married Sir John Barnard and came to live in the Abington area. But with her death all trace of them vanished.

Did she perhaps hide them for safety's sake during her own lifetime and die without revealing their hiding place? She lived at Abington during a time when the theatre was in disgrace. The Cromwellian and Puritanical regime was at its height; the theatres were closed, and anyone with theatrical connections such as Elizabeth had was certainly not anxious to advertise the fact.

Whatever the truth may be, the mystery still awaits its detective. Where is Lady Barnard's coffin? Where are the famous papers? It is a problem for one of the great heroes of detective fiction, and both fortune and world-wide fame await anyone who can unravel it.

Old Corn Exchange Wellingborough, now replaced by a supermarket

Wellingborough

Wellingborough has a compact charm, an attractive clean brightness of red brick houses mingled with rich old ironstone buildings that makes it one of Northamptonshire's most pleasant towns. Apart from a few of the usual ominous signs of the dragon of modern development it is retaining its natural character remarkably well.

Discounting, for example, the new technical college poking its nose up over All Hallows' lovely spire and churchyard, and a piece of aggressive modernism clapped onto the handsome old council office frontage in Swanspool, there is not much so far to complain of in the town centre.

The Golden Lion inn, with its over-sailing gable – the sort of building foreigners dream of as the typical English mediaeval tavern – is fortunately still unspoiled. It has a fine lounge with an antique gallery resembling a miniature Oxford college dining hall. The Tudor Cottages nearby, and the great Tithe Barn, are other ancient gems redolent of Wellingborough's pleasant past. So is the Hind Hotel, a superb piece of gabled golden stone, comfortably suggesting Wellingborough's days as a spa when no less a person than Charles the First's Queen, Henrietta Maria, is said to have come to drink the waters there.

The centre is dominated by the Parish Church of All Hallows, flanked by attractive old brownstone buildings and the prettily Gothicised rectory close by. It

The Golden Lion, Wellingborough

retains its old bells that play a tune every few hours, though they don't always seem to function when I visit the town.

The interior of the church is richly rewarding. An amalgam of artistic monuments awaits the visitor, ranging from some fine mediaeval miserere stalls to a colourful Victorian east window and three interesting, though somewhat violent, modern windows, including one by John Piper and another by Evie Hone. There is also a wall painting by Hans Feibusch well worth seeing.

But for the selective connoisseur the outstanding treasure of Wellingborough is, of course, the magnificent Edwardian masterpiece of Sir Ninian Comper, St. Mary's Church, down against the railway station. I have mentioned before this superb fantasy in blue and gold, with its solemn ironstone fabric and its noble tower. Inside its grace, its lightness, its wonderful lifting of the Gothic style on to the exuberant plane of Viennese Baroque or Austrian Rococo, never fails to enchant. Everything in it bespeaks joy in life; there is nothing of religious gloom here, nothing but delight in

Vaulting in the Porch, All Hallows Wellingborough

colour and gold and glittering glass. Still not finished in its internal decorative scheme there is enough completed to give a breathtaking idea of what it will one day be like.

Wellingborough, however, has other subtleties beside its obvious main sights. I often go there looking for antiques and have had several rewards, including a handsome blue and gold Regency vase, three feet tall, and a fine ormolu and porcelain-panelled clock.

Then there are interesting open spaces, a whole chain of them, in fact, ranging from Bassett's Close down to the fields below Wellingborough School. My favourite of these, macabre though the choice may sound, is the romantic cemetery which has a wealth of evergreens and two exquisite chapels with beautiful spires and nicely carved gargoyles. They are a most fetching little pair of Victoriana and in autumn when their crimson creeper shines in the sun they are doubly charming.

Shopping in Wellingborough is good, and I profoundly hope the town will not spoil its attractive main streets with a rash of ugly chain stores if its proposed expansion scheme comes to fruition. Its shops at present have some nice touches, like the dome reminiscent of a bit of Edwardian Moscow over the former Granville Hotel, and a pretty bit of Edwardiana with black and white timbering which is now a chemist's shop.

Finally, there is a most interesting oval-shaped Congregational Church in the High Street which is probably unique in design. It is in the golden-brown stone which adorns so much of Wellingborough and is a handsome reminder of the careful building techniques of a century ago, solid, unhurried, built to please and built to last.

Church and Trees at Bugbrooke

Trees

One of Northamptonshire's greatest county treasures lies in its magnificent and, alas, often too-little-regarded ancient trees.

"An honest man's the noblest work of God", wrote Pope, but he might have added to that a really superb and fully matured tree. And another eighteenth century poet, our own (or nearly own!) Cowper of Olney, North Bucks. said, in a much-quoted line "God made the country and man made the town", but, as far as the English countryside is concerned, this is only partly ture. For the actual arrangement of the countryside, and especially the planting of its wonderful clumps and masses of trees, has been largely directed by our ancestors who laid out our counties with fields and hedgerows and those magnificent trees which so often give character to a piece of parkland or lonely country lane.

Northamptonshire is especially rich in fine "treescapes". Woods we have in plenty; some huge and almost primeval, like Badby Wood and the remains of Whittlebury and Salcey Forests, still very extensive. Others are charmingly miniature, yet romantic and mysterious enough at sunset or under the harvest moon. Delapre Wood, so close to Northampton and not nearly enough prized for the treasure it is, with its enchanting view over the town and down the river valley, is one of the more exquisite of the

Trees at Lamport Hall (copyright Country Life)

miniatures. And even Abington Park has its own pretty little wood, hardly more than a spinney, but with at least one magnificent tree in it, that splendid triple-trunked chestnut close to the stream which I always call the Trinity Tree.

Have you noticed how often, and with what subconscious art, our ancestors set their country cottages and tall-gabled farmhouses against a background of rich dark trees? Of course, we at present are seeing these lovely vistas at their best since the trees have now come to their full maturity after perhaps two hundred years or more; Abington Park, for example, can never have looked more beautiful than it now looks after several centuries of slow growth. This was one of the reasons why there was rightly so much outcry a few years ago about any attempt to interfere with it. It has a particularly fine sweep of flowering chestnut trees along the road which leads between its two parts, and if there are ever any proposals to cut this avenue down I hope opinion will rise against them.

One of the most famous avenues of trees in the county is the stupendous approach to Castle Ashby which recalls the world's greatest triumph of the tree-planter's art, the Park at Versailles. And Boughton House, near Weekley, still has much to show of the work of "Planter John" who consciously strove to emulate Versailles and created at Boughton perhaps the nearest English approach to it.

But when all is said I don't think that for exquisite beauty you can beat some of the simple effects achieved in village after village of our county though now, alas, so often disturbed by those "developments" that are throttling the beauty of England everywhere. There are some entrancing tree and village ensembles at, for instance, Newnham (my own ancestral village), Kislingbury, and a specially fine composition, the churchyard and church at Bugbrooke.

So let us at all costs beware of the Tree Chopper, beware of him who shouts out loud "Who cares about a lot of old trees anyway?" The answer, of course, is that everybody who loves one of England's finest and most precious possessions cares about them, for they have taken long, slow ages to mature and should not therefore be lightly slaughtered in a couple of hours.

Landscape at Boughton House (copyright Country Life)

Easton Neston

Easton Neston has been called the finest house of its date in England. It is certainly a triumph of exquisite architectural taste, even though the cool classical perfection of Hawksmoor's design might seem more at home in France than in the essentially romantic countryside of Northamptonshire.

Easton Neston is, in fact, an enchanting essay in the manner of Versailles, but all in miniature, and it would have made a perfect setting for one of Watteau's "Fetes Galantes" or one of Boucher's glittering allegorical fantasies.

The classical style, with its insistence on orderly symmetry and the "correct" disposition of all ornamental features such as columns, pilasters and pediments, never took real root in England, though there are many superb examples of it, such as Lamport Hall and Vanbrugh's masterpiece at Blenheim Palace. The real genius of the English is more for picturesque, asymmetrical, slightly rambling compositions, such as the great Gothic churches and charming little towns like our own Brackley and Towcester.

But England's Classical Age, blossoming with Inigo Jones and flowering with Christopher Wren, Vanbrugh and Hawksmoor, was none the less a very splendid chapter of English building. And nowhere is there a more handsome example of it than at Easton Neston.

Built around 1702 for Sir William Fermor, it was Hawksmoor's first completely original work, for he had worked in collaboration with Wren for many years, and Wren had indeed been consulted about Easton Neston as far back as about 1682. Both Wren and Vanbrugh no doubt influenced Hawksmoor; he had collaborated with Vanbrugh at the spectacular Castle Howard a few years earlier. But the design has a distinctive quality which marks it out as Hawksmoor's own.

Hawksmoor was a man of immensely varied talents. It is a fascinating study to compare, for example, the serene classical

Above: Easton Neston, West Facade

Right: Easton Neston, Main Staircase (copyright Country Life)

Easton Neston, Drawing Room

splendour of Easton Neston with his oddly romantic twin towers at All Souls' college, Oxford, highly picturesque and Gothic in spirit. They look forward to the Romantic Revival, to Beckford's Fonthill and even to St. Pancras Station! It was Hawksmoor, too, who added the two Gothic western towers to Westminster Abbey which blend so admirably with its general style that visitors to London have been deceived into thinking them part of the original building.

Easton Neston is completely stone-faced, the stone being of a particularly beautiful quality from the Helmdon quarries. It is not a large house as Northamptonshire mansions go, only a Lilliput to the Brobdingnag of Burghley or Castle Ashby. But for perfection of line and detail the superb western facade is probably unsurpassed anywhere, unless by Gabriel's exquisite composition of the Petit Trianon. The front owes much of its distinction to the splendid Corinthian pilasters and the magnificently controlled frieze and balustrade above. This frieze embodies the motto of the Fermors "Hora e Sempre".

The interior of this lovely house has undergone considerable remodelling since Hawksmoor's time, but it contains a wealth of fine decorative features. Prominent among these are the great staircase with an exquisite wrought iron balustrade and the wonderful adornments of the Drawing Room which is elaborately embellished with stucco panels of superlative quality.

Lamport Hall

Like Easton Neston Lamport is an outstanding product of the classical age of English domestic architecture. Its central core, the nucleus of the present house, is earlier than Easton Neston by some 50 years and dates from around 1654; it was the work of John Webb, the famous pupil of the even more famous Inigo Jones.

The finely designed wings, which extended Webb's frontage to more than twice its former length, were added by Francis Smith of Warwick in excellent and restrained taste, and still in the cool Palladian style of the original. This addition was almost exactly contemporary with the handsome rebuilding of what is now Abington Park Museum, also by Francis Smith. It dates from 1732–41 and was a model of what such an extension should be.

Later additions were made in the 19th century and it is remarkable that during the full flood of the Victorian Gothic Revival when buildings were being Gothicised and Elizabethanised and Tudorised all over England, Lamport itself escaped almost unscathed. It remains an extremely beautiful, restful and collected design, un-English in the sense that all classical houses seem to suggest Renaissance Italy rather than the quiet English countryside, but none the less beautiful for that. The lovely long white stone facade, seen from the Northampton to Leicester road, and approached by the delightful gates added by Hakewill in the early 19th century, is one of Northamptonshire's finest sights.

The entire ensemble is, of course, enormously aided by its magnificent position. To the west lies the superb valley landscape, varied, colourful and dramatic, suggesting the Dales of Derbyshire rather than the usually placid Northamptonshire scene. And away on the horizon rises the spire of the county's most famous church, the seventh century basilican Brixworth which has been described as the finest monument of its date north of the Alps.

Into this marvellously beautiful scene the Lamport group, hall, church and rectory, fits with that unerring skill with which English builders of the past, unlike those of today, managed to combine their differing styles. Francis Smith, for instance, produced a most serene design for the rectory, suggesting even more strongly this time the style of Abington Museum. Its golden stone contrasts delightfully with the snowy splendour of the Hall.

The adjoining church is far older than either rectory or hall, but it blends in with them remarkably well. It is also a most interesting living history book of ecclesiastical styles, ranging from the Norman tower and some 13th century features to a rare piece of late 17th century work in the north chapel. The Victorian window of 1847 is an astonishing specimen and well worth seeing.

There are some fine features inside the Hall which the Ishams, who have lived at Lamport since 1560, have preserved with meticulous care and impeccable taste. They include some splendid pictures, chimney pieces and plasterwork and reflect in their stately serenity the calm excellence of the outside.

There may be larger and more overpowering architectural ensembles, even in Northamptonshire itself, than the Lamport group, but perhaps nowhere is there one more perfectly expressive of the varied story of English country life, or one more perfectly integrated with its setting.

Lamport Hall (both copyright Country Life)

Famous Stained Glass at Middleton Cheney

Detail of William Morris Window

Victorian stained glass has never had much of a reputation in artistic circles, but the recent revival of interest in Victoriana has made many people begin to take a second look at some of the finer examples. And Northamptonshire possesses, as it happens, one of the most famous collections of Victorian church windows in all England, the splendid group by the Morris firm at Middleton Cheney.

The church in which they are housed is itself beautiful, with a finely proportioned tower and spire that dominates the landscape for miles around. But the Morris windows, inserted during the rectorship of the Rev. Buckley, are its chief glory and well worthy of a pilgrimage for anyone interested in fine stained glass.

William Morris was, of course, the prime mover in that great artistic revival of craftsmanship in the 19th century which sought to replace the tyranny of machine-made work with a return to the tradition of the medieval guilds and hand-made objects. For Morris and his fellow artists in the Pre-Raphaelite Movement the Middle Ages were a shining lamp of artistic achievement to which they constantly turned for inspiration. Morris was enormously influential in all branches of the arts and his lovely home at Kelmscott Manor in Oxfordshire ultimately became the centre of a complete artistic crusade. Fine printing, wallpapers, textiles, poetry, painting and stained glass windows all poured from the Morris firm, and the Middleton Cheney glass is an epitome of the joint achievement of Morris and his friends.

The Rev. Buckley, who commissioned the work, was a friend of Sir Edward Burne-Jones, the great Pre-Raphaelite painter, and in 1864-65 he inserted the magnificent east window which was a combined work by Morris himself, Burne-Jones, Philip Webb, Ford Madox Brown, and a lesser known artist, S. Solomon.

The exact contribution made by each artist has been a matter of some controversy, but there seems no doubt that Morris designed the figures of Eve and the various holy virgins; the Adoration of the Lamb and St. Alban being by Burne-Jones and the Four Beasts and some of the angels by Philip Webb.

The whole window is a kind of biblical pageant which includes the Tribes of the Apocalypse, Adam, Noah, David, Isaiah,

St. Peter, St. Paul, St. Augustine, St. Catherine, Abraham, Moses, Eve, the Madonna, St. Marỳ Magdalene, St. John, St. Alban and St. Agnes.

But there are other windows besides this great centre-piece, including a particularly splendid west window by Burne-Jones showing the three young men in the fiery furnace with a background of remarkable and very beautiful yellow glass.

Other windows were added at various dates between 1865 and 1880, and they include Old Testament and Gospel panels, two later ones in the chancel being a memorial to Buckley himself.

These wonderful windows should certainly' be seen not only by those who already admire the best in Victorian art, but by any who are still prone to dismiss Victorian stained glass as unworthy of attention. They will rapidly convert the doubters as well as delight the connoisseurs.

As an aperitif for anyone prepared to take the trouble, pay a visit to St. Sepulchre's Church at Northampton. St. Sepulchre's has also a fine piece of Victorian glass in the North Chapel window by Kempe, another excellent glass artist whose work was often on as high a level as that of the Middleton Cheney craftsmen.

While in Middleton Cheney church, notice the canopy of the rood screen which is of interest to amateurs of Victoriana. It is by Sir Gilbert Scott, the most prolific of all the Victorian church architects, who did some restoration work here in the 1860's. The ceilings of the nave and chancel, painted about 1460, were restored under the direction of Scott in 1865. These are very much admired by those who raise their eyes, but missed by most casual viewers of the church.

Scott, incidentally, was born only just over the border, in Buckinghamshire, and his very first building was in Northamptonshire, the vicarage at Wappenham, designed for his father, the Rev. Scott, in the 1830's.

Right: The East Window at Middleton Cheney

David
Isaiah
S Peter
S Paul
S Austin
S Catherine

Solomon and the Queen of Sheba

In this chapter, instead of selecting one of Northamptonshire's traditional treasures, I am choosing one of its recently acquired possessions, the Damini painting which now hangs in the Northampton Central Art Gallery in Guildhall Road.

The Central Gallery, in spite of its unattractive exterior and cramped exhibiting space, makes up in quality for what it lacks in quantity and almost all of its small permanent collection is of high merit. And the Damini painting of Solomon and the Queen of Sheba is one of the gallery's most spectacular finds in recent years. Along with the seventeenth century royal cabinet purchased in 1916, it makes a fine addition to the treasures of the town.

Not much is known about Damini, but he lived in London for a time and it is possible, indeed probable, that he heard some of Handel's music for inevitably as you contemplate this picture you recall the famous "Arrival of the Queen of Sheba" from Handel's "Solomon" which dates from around the same time.

The painter's conception of the biblical incident is Baroque, even Rococo, certainly theatrical; it is worked out as a piece of staging and bears little or no relation to what the original Solomon and the Queen of Sheba must have looked like. The Queen herself appears as a kind of prima donna or ballerina, half operatic, half terpsichore, while the King spreads his hands out in a theatrical gesture of welcome to this fairy-like visitant who is accompanied by a stock of gifts that also look like stage properties from some eighteenth century opera.

The painting is sympathetically mounted in a gilded frame of great charm which suggests the proscenium of a little opera house in the Austria of Maria Theresa or the France of Louis the Fifteenth.

Of course, to those who demand truth to nature or stark realism or intellectual expressionism from painting such a picture will be anathema. The figures are not the genuine human beings of Rembrandt or the passionately conceived creatures of El Greco. They are simply brilliant puppets dancing at the whim of the artist and as such are undoubtedly artificial. But it has to be remembered that much great art is artificial and often bears little or no relation to life as it is lived by the majority of human beings. The operas of Mozart, the architecture of Wren and the poetry of Keats are all "artificial" to a degree when contrasted, for instance, with the severe real-life "functionalism" of today.

The artists of the rococo age, the age which gave the world the finest porcelain from Sèvres and the great palaces of France and Vienna such as Versailles and Schönbrunn, were mainly concerned with creating works which were intended to be primarily ornamental. They aimed at perfection of grouping and colour, at brilliance of effect. They wished to give pleasure to the beholder rather than to give expression to the deeper things of life or to pose any abstruse intellectual questions.

It is with this in mind that the Damini "Queen of Sheba" must be judged, simply, in fact, as a piece of brilliant decoration, like a fine carpet or a handsome article of

Damini's Solomon and the Queen of Sheba

furniture or a lovely Dresden vase. If you approach it in this spirit you must admit that it is a masterpiece of its school and Northampton is extremely fortunate to have acquired so exquisite an example of this little known artist's work.

It is only of recent years that the Museum has been able to spread its wings financially and make the permanent collection really worthy of a town the size of Northampton.

The Damini is my own favourite of everything that has been acquired in the post-war period, but there are now a growing number of other important works, such as the Verrio design for the "Heaven" room at Burghley, a fine Pannini classical-ruins composition, and a good Fontebasso.

In fact, the main section in the gallery upstairs, which has been attractively lined with pale green brocade and given several interesting pieces of furniture, including a splendid Italian marriage-chest, is at last a corner of Northampton where one can really feel oneself in the "capital city" of a county that cares about culture.

Boughton House, North Front

Boughton House

Northamptonshire is fortunate in its great classical houses such as Althorp, Easton Neston and Lamport Hall. They were all products of the period when the rambling Gothic Manors of the late Middle Ages had gone out of fashion and every nobleman had begun to aspire to "correctness" and classical order in his home. At that time also the great squares and streets of London were beginning to be laid out in orderly style, and classical elegance in the manner of the Versailles court of France became the guiding principle in aristocratic domestic life, as much for the country mansion as for the city home.

Northamptonshire was to possess one of the most French-looking pieces of classical architecture in all England in the magnificent north front of Boughton House, near Kettering, the work of the First Duke of Montagu. This highly gifted man had been British Ambassador in Paris in the later years of the 17th century and had obviously imbibed French ideas from the splendid court of the "Sun King" to which he was accredited. It is curious that two centuries later the Baron de Rothschild was similarly to build in the hills of Buckinghamshire his equally lavish French-style chateau at Waddesdon. By that time, however, the taste was for riotous ornament in building

Right: State Room at Boughton House (copyright Country Life)

and Waddesdon is just as ornate as Boughton is classically restrained.

It was the First Duke of Montagu also who built the essentially French Montagu House in London on the site of the present British Museum, and his name was commemorated in the nearby Montagu Street.

The North Front of Boughton is so thoroughly French in spirit that it could easily be taken for the facade of the mansion of some wealthy Marquis of the Pompadour era. Emerging from its perfectly proportioned court one can visualise the gilded rococo coaches and richly painted sedan chairs of pre-Revolutionary France; the building is like a splendid ghost from that epoch of powdered wigs and gold snuff-boxes, fans and three cornered hats. Modern clothes and the bustle of cars seem strangely alien to its serene majesty and it presents a coolly handsome but slightly scornful face to the prosaic 20th century.

Inside there are sumptuous painted ceilings by Verrio and Cheron, and several interesting chimney-pieces some of which date from Tudor times. The magnificent collection of furniture and works of art in the state rooms includes tapestries, fine carpets, and some choice Italian and English paintings by notable masters.

Near at hand is the lovely village of Weekley, still a haven of charm, and around the house lie the remains of the great park which was laid out by the Second Duke, known as "John the Planter", along the lines of the famous park at Versailles. Not far off is the church of Warkton, celebrated for its masterpieces of 18th century sculpture, all monuments to the Montagus, including groups by Van Gelder and Roubiliac of remarkable grandeur.

They make up the finest collection of church sculpture in Northamptonshire, and indeed one of the most impressive to be found in any village church in England.

Boughton House, I must point out, is not open to the public.

Presented by the Friends of the Art Gallery

17th Century Spanish Royal Cabinet
This cabinet has seventeen drawers ornamented with episodes from Don Quixote executed in ivory and scarlet tortoiseshell. The central feature opens to reveal a hall, chequer-paved with ebony and ivory and with a carved ceiling, the walls being five arcaded mirrors and the whole enclosed by engraved ivory twisted pilasters. Dated 1653, the designs are the work of the master Diego de Medina. There is an inlaid portrait of Cervantes and the arched top bears the arms of Philip IV of Spain. The sides of the cabinet and the inside of the door are faced with parqueterie.

The Spanish Royal Cabinet

I wrote earlier about the Damini painting of Solomon and the Queen of Sheba, recently acquired by Northampton Art Gallery and Museum. Another of its acquisitions which certainly qualifies for the title of a County Treasure is the splendid 17th century Spanish Royal Cabinet, designed by Diego de Medina and purchased a few years ago.

This magnificent object helps to fill a definite gap in the exhibits of the museum which is not rich in articles of furniture and has much needed a few pieces of this quality to supplement its rapidly growing collection of paintings and china.

The 17th century in Europe was a great age of furniture craftsmen, and it is well known that in France there was an efflorescence of genius in the work of Boulle and other artists at the court of Louis XIV. But France was obviously not alone in fine furnishings, as this wonderful Spanish example clearly shows. Its origins are well documented by the inscription on the front which gives the name of its designer as Diego de Medina and its date as 1653. The entire work is a most elaborate and delicately wrought triumph of tortoiseshell inlay on wood, with brass fittings and cresting, depicting in 16 panels scenes from Cervantes' "Don Quixote".

The grace and refinement of these panels are already a long way from the comparative heaviness of earlier 17th century work (as evinced in some of our own Jacobean woodwork), and they look forward to the elegance of the 18th century, an elegance never surpassed in the entire history of furniture.

The base of the cabinet, with its finely turned legs, is apparently of a later date, but what must strike everyone who examines the piece is the astonishingly perfect condition of the cabinet itself, its delicate inlaid panels looking as if they were made yesterday rather than over 300 years ago.

The Don Quixote panels surround an ingenious central inner cabinet, beautifully framed by miniature columns, This portion opens to show an arrangement of concealed mirrors which would give the royal owner an opportunity of observing if anyone were approaching from behind his back with criminal intent.

The panels themselves depict some of the best known episodes in Cervantes' famous novel, including the Don tilting at windmills under the impression that they were giants. Others show Sancho being tossed in a blanket, the adventure at the inn, the encounter with the strolling players and the Wagon of Death, and the episodes of the chained prisoners and the lion in its cage. A central panel shows Don Quixote and Sancho Panza, and another is a portrait of Cervantes himself.

The cabinet came from Vienna and is an interesting example of the cultural ties of the Royal House of Austria with Spain, a country which they had inherited by marriage.

There is no doubt that the acquisition of this piece was most discriminating on the part of the museum, and it was also purchased at an extremely modest price for so fine a specimen.

Church Towers of the County

In another article I wrote about the Spires of Northamptonshire and pointed out that the Towers of the county's churches are, in fact, far more numerous than its Spires. But the towers are, on the whole, much less famous than the spires, though there are many which deserve a greater celebrity than they have ever found.

Generally, the towers predominate in the western part of the county and the spires in the east, especially in the Nene Valley around Oundle, but there are many exceptions to this grouping. And, as it happens, the most magnificent of all Northamptonshire's church towers, that glorious late medieval work at Titchmarsh, is itself right up in the "spire country", just beyond Thrapston. It comes as a superb contrast to the glittering cluster of masterpieces of the spire builder's art which adorn all that part of the river-land which lies towards the Huntingdonshire border.

Titchmarsh has been called the finest parish church tower in England outside Somerset, and that is indeed high praise. For Somerset, of course, is the Mecca of church tower architecture just as Northamptonshire is the Mecca of spires. We are therefore specially lucky to have this graceful and splendidly proportioned tower along with the famous spires of the surrounding district. It is a later example of mediaeval art, belonging clearly to the Perpendicular Period, though the actual dating of it is a matter of conjecture.

Equally beautiful in its more slender way is the golden-brown loveliness of Whiston, set on its own lonely hillside. Richly decorated with quatrefoils, pinnacles and gargoyles, it glows with a fascinating deep yellow of its own in the afternoon or evening sunlight. It was probably the last church to be built in England before the Reformation, its date being around 1534, and it looks straight across the valley to its far older companion, the most famous of all Northamptonshire's towers, the 1,000 year old Earls Barton.

Earls Barton tower is the grandest surviving specimen of Anglo Saxon architecture in the country and has probably been illustrated in more books on architecture than anything else Northamptonshire possesses.

All three of the towers so far mentioned are very well known. But what of the lesser-known examples, towers which so plentifully sprinkle the quiet Northamptonshire countryside?

Many of them have a remarkable rightness in their particular position, often set on river slopes or hillsides, and backed by great masses of trees against which they stand out exquisitely in the light of the sun or moon. How finely, for instance, Cogenhoe tower sits on its hill as you come in from the east by boat along the Nene; how serenely Little Houghton rises above the housetops of its village! And how pleasantly Towcester's tall brown tower comes into view as you turn off from the

Left to right:
Castle Ashby Church
St Laurence's Towcester
All Saints' Earls Barton

main street and approach its green garden-like churchyard!

There are indeed so many of the unsung village towers of our county which have their own charm that only a few can be mentioned here. Badby, for example, close to the darkly mysterious Badby Wood; St. Giles' of Northampton, a very good town church which is not nearly well enough appreciated by local people; Castle Ashby, brilliantly set against the superb Tudor background of the great house and its lovely gardens.

Then there are interesting "saddle-back" towers like Rothersthorpe, and fine "lantern" towers like Lowick and Fotheringhay; strange and exotic-looking towers like Irthlingborough and homely, dumpy little towers like Weston Favell. Sometimes you can trace a family resemblance between two distant towers; attractively suggestive of Whiston is that far too little known but very beautiful Perpendicular tower of Marston Trussell, right away on the edge of Leicestershire.

The variety of our towers is enormous and the styles of building of every conceivable kind; beautiful at all times of the year, whether under sun or snow.

Left to right:
St Mary's Titchmarsh
St Mary's Whiston
St Peter's Cogenhoe
St Giles' Northampton

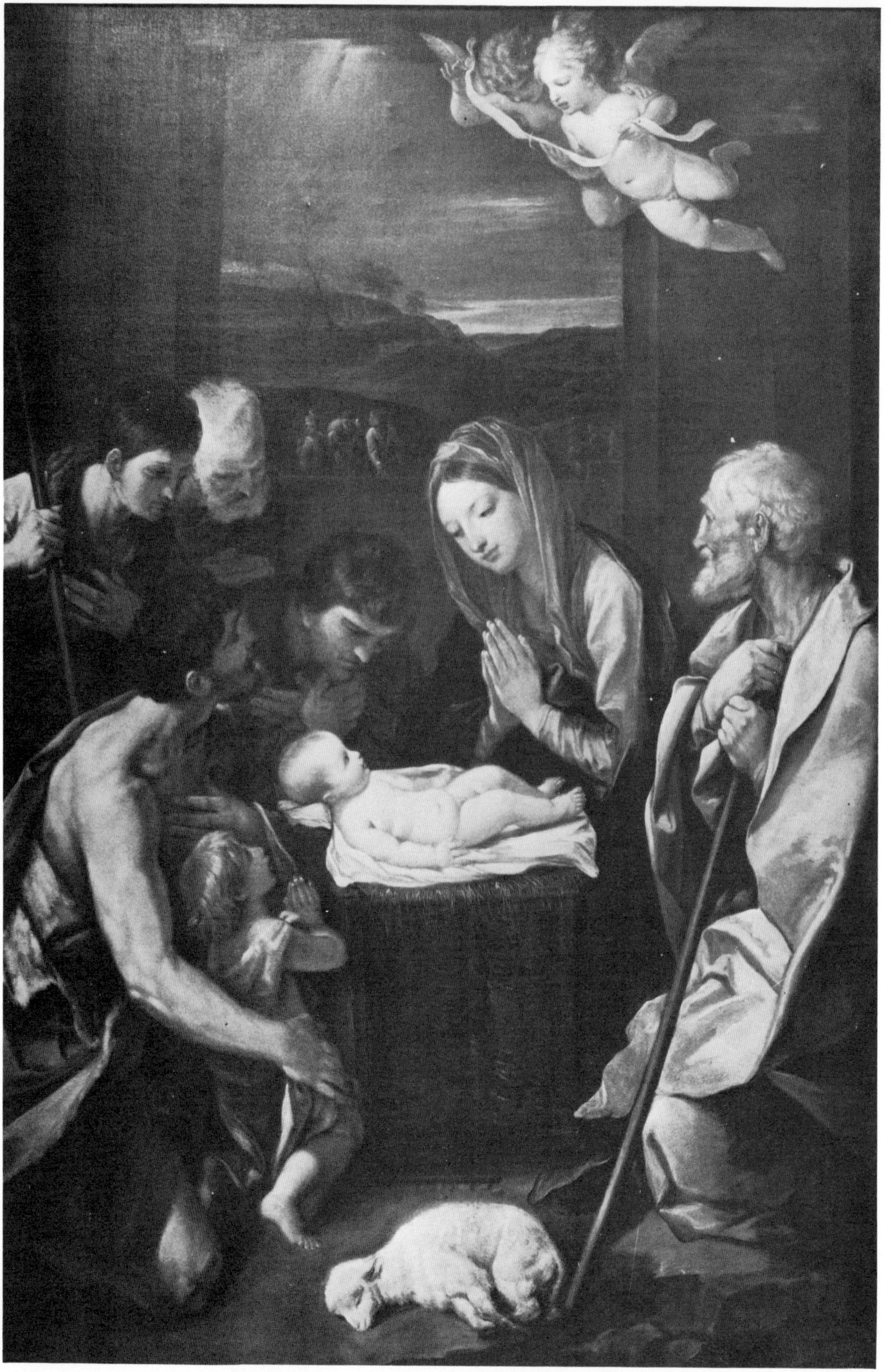

Angry Artist - Serene Virgin

Northampton is indebted to Sir Gyles Isham for many things, and not least for his generosity in exhibiting at the Central Art Gallery so comprehensive a collection of paintings, books and manuscripts from his ancestral home at Lamport Hall. In 1969 he added to this a further extended loan to the gallery of one of the finest pictures in his possession, the magnificent Guido Reni "Adoration of the Shepherds".

The exhibition was mainly of items brought back from Rome by Sir Thomas Isham who anticipated the 18th century fashion for making "the Grand Tour" of Europe as early as 1676. This painting, however, was a later addition to the Lamport collection and seems to have been acquired by the seventh Baronet, Sir Justinian Isham, who succeeded to the title in 1772.

It is a splendid example of the great Italian artists's work, richly but softly coloured, superbly composed and full of an exquisite tenderness, a tenderness largely concentrated in the lovely Madonna herself. With an echo of the classical perfection of Botticelli's masterly studies of the female face it has a more richly personal quality so that the divine and the human are beautifully blended in this half-angelic half-human figure. She kneels in softly lighted splendour before the Crib, the central character of the group surrounding the Holy Child, with a pair of small but finely conceived angels in the sky beyond. The rough masculinity of the shepherds contrasts with the refined grace of this delicate yet firm Virgin, so different from some of the cold featured and hard-looking Madonnas of earlier Italian and Byzantine art.

Guido Reni has indeed been accused of sentimentality in some of his religious pictures, but sentiment is here transmuted into a calm but radiant ecstasy.

This excellent painter, usually known simply as "Guido", was a contemporary of Shakespeare, born only nine years later and outliving him by some years until his

Left: Reni's Adoration of the Shepherds

death in 1642. His world was therefore that of the late Renaissance merging into the early Baroque period, a world still full of the violence and drama reflected in Shakespeare's plays and later recalled in Verdi's operas "Rigoletto" and "Don Carlos". He was born in Bologna, in 1575, the city famous for its ancient University, the oldest in Europe, and for its fine food. And it was back to Bologna that Guido, after a long and at times tempestuous career in Rome and elsewhere, retired finally to die during the period when England was in the grips of the Civil War.

It would be pleasant to think that the artist who conceived this lovely, calmly ecstatic interpretation of the Nativity of Christ had a life as serene as his approach to it seems to indicate. The reverse, however, must have been the case, and his brilliant talent apparently provoked professional jealously so fierce that he was even once threatened with murder by a fellow artist. This was Caravaggio, who, however, was always in trouble with the Italian police owing to his violent and ungovernable temper.

Guido himself seems also to have had a quarrelsome, though noble personality, and there are records of angry disputes with the Pope's treasurer and with his patrons in Naples where he painted the frescoes of the church of S. Gennaro. He died in financial straits, having been apparently a confirmed gambler for many years, and one of his creditors is said to have sat, watch in hand, forcing him to do work by the hour in settlement of his debts.

Guido's reputation, after attacks by the romanticists of Ruskin's time, has revived during the present century, and he is now seen again as one of the greatest Italian painters of the late Renaissance. It is interesting that the National Gallery in London has recently acquired a larger canvas by Reni on the same subject as this "Adoration of the Shepherds". It almost seems as if this might be a smaller study for the National Gallery painting, so similar is the general composition of the figures.

This, however, is nothing more than conjecture and in any case Northampton is fortunate to have an opportunity of admiring this enchanting work.

Northampton Market Square

Northampton Market Square

Ruinous demolitions have taken place on the Market Square since this essay was written, destroying much of its former charm. Especially unnecessary was the destruction of the fine Victorian Fountain and the demolition of the graceful facade of the Peacock Hotel.

But, as with the essay on "Taverns of the Town", I have left what follows in its original form since it was written when the Square was still looking at its most charming.

Fortunately, one really excellent building has been added recently, the delightful yellow stone offices at present occupied by the Northampton Development Corporation. This is easily the best building erected in Northampton during the last forty years.

I was reading "Sketches by Boz" again the other day, and I thought how Dickens would have loved our Market Square. How he would have painted it in all lights and at all times, foggy November mornings, bright April afternoons, golden September evenings. What vivid pictures he would have left of its Wednesday and Saturday metamorphosis from a dignified, quiet and half-empty square into a streaming, jostling, fascinating clutter of merchandise and miscellaneous humanity. First he would probably have transported his reader to the North side and described the exquisite vista from the Parade with its attics, Fountain, Georgian and Regency buildings and the left-hand corner glimpse of the white stone County Hall and the brown stone eighteenth century Judge's Lodgings.

Then, by small gradations, he would have drawn us into the life of the Market itself, with its early morning carts lumbering in from the distant villages, its piles of apples and grapes catching the first beams of the morning sun, its deepening crescendo of animation during the day, on to the last flicker of the acetylene lamps and the mountain of paper litter to be cleared up in the evenings when the stalls come down.

I have seen many markets in Europe and the East, in Italy, in Lisbon, in India, in Baghdad. But our Market Square is, I think, the most beautiful I have encountered. It is, of course, now the largest in England. Until the conversion of Nottingham Market into what the people of Nottingham call "Slab Square" we had to be content with second place in point of size, but there was never, surely, any serious rivalry in actual beauty between us and Nottingham.

For ours is a perfect square, with the atmosphere of a piece of Brussels or Rouen, and admirably arranged so that there is an entrance to each corner without breaking up the pleasant line of buildings on each side.

It must, of course, originally have been even more beautiful than it is today. For the Parade side has been entirely rebuilt, and though the buildings are quite good of their kind they tend to spoil the harmony of the rest of the Square. The Eastern side has also suffered somewhat, but both the South and the West sides are quite perfect. One of the loveliest pieces of all is Drury Chambers, with its beautiful pilasters, fine proportions and delightful old roof. But it is rivalled by its next-door neighbour. This charming house has kept to perfection the atmosphere, the very patina of an eighteenth century print and its recent redecoration and cleaning has happily preserved this air of a vanished elegance.

Like a central pivot, a kingpin around which the merry-go-round of the Market revolves, rises the much-criticised Victorian Fountain, proudly displaying its date, 1863. Personally, I think the Fountain beautiful, and should hotly protest if it were ever removed. Once it had a fine old lamp surmounting its central shaft which shed a solemn yellow gaslight over the Square. Was it broken up, I wonder, or does it linger still in some old cellar, like that honest old lamp in Hans Andersen's entrancing story which went into honourable retirement to give light to an aged couple who lived in a basement?

What the Fountain has looked down on! The visit of King George the Fifth and Queen Mary, for example, in 1913. Proclamations, rallies, religious orators predicting hellfire for all, political orators shouting that the millennium is only round the corner if you will but vote for them and their party. Carnivals (I remember one years ago when pasteboard Gates of the Town were erected and Quainte Olde Northampton brought to life again with a vengeance), bands, bus-tour queues, travelling exhibitions and seas of cars.

But of course the apotheosis, the nirvana of all good Market Squares is the Market itself, and no doubt the Fountain views this with greater affection than anything else. The Market is very efficiently organised and

HALIFAX BUILDING SOCIETY
Buswell
XJF 504J

conducted, and the new metal frames for the stalls are certainly a great improvement on the old wooden poles.

But I regret the passing of the pleasant orange and green striped awnings which used to flaunt themselves à la française in the Spring breeze, though no doubt they finally fluttered into picturesque tatters and had to be replaced. However, there is little time for sentimental regrets in a Wednesday or Saturday promenade, for there is always a positive microcosm of human commerce to be investigated and sampled.

Fruit and flowers, azaleas, daffodils massed in golden regiments against bright green paper wrappings, mimosa, tulips or chrysanthemums according to the season, second-hand books from Victorian poets to Baroness Orczy, Western Magazines blazing red and yellow as the dragoons in "Carmen", antiques, curios, Chinese ginger-jars, framed pictures and bedroom texts such as that terrible Eye that follows one all round the room, with "Thou, God, Seest Me" inscribed beneath.

Then the billows, the waves, the piled-up oceans of coloured materials, prints, chintz, tapestry, cretonne. Next there may be lampshades, candlesticks and an old cylinder gramophone cheek by jowl with cushions and crockery, teapots, good and frightful, ornaments, charming and the reverse. And inevitably there turn up here those heavy and lugubrious china dogs that finally stare at one from their last resting place in front room windows, and that eternal china child dangling cherries over his mouth who is always displayed, when he reaches home, looking out into the street and never in on the occupants of the room.

Undoubtedly Dickens should have left us a picture of this swarming Market Square, for he would have done it so well. And Arnold Bennett also could have made it live permanently and pulsate through his pages, just as he transfixed for ever the clock towers and stations and trams and people of the Five Towns in his brilliant work.

Northampton certainly awaits its novelist, the material is all here in its ancient thoroughfares, its long history and its modern industrial prosperity. Let us hope it will not have to wait much longer, and any aspirant might well make a start with a story circling around the Market Square.

Market Square, Northampton

Ancient Churches of Northampton

The town centre of Northampton is at present undergoing such a carnival of demolition and reconstruction that whole sections of it are rapidly becoming unrecognisable, even to those who knew the place up to a few months ago.

But amid the chaos of dust and rubble and the wilderness of half knocked down streets to the north of the Market Square certain ancient features stand firm to remind the visitor of the important historical city which once Northampton was.

The mediaeval walls which made of it a fine circular city have now been entirely replaced by modern streets, still running in a roughly circular form, like the famous Ringstrasse in Vienna. And in the centre of the circle All Saints' Church, as in centuries past, still forms the pivotal point of the town, while the other ancient churches, St. Peter's, Holy Sepulchre, St. John's and St. Giles', remain from mediaeval times at what were originally the west, north, south and east exits from the town.

And anyone who wishes to get a general idea of the mediaeval lay-out of Northampton can easily do this by visiting these five churches, for the streets connecting them are the main arteries of the town centre.

All Saints' will inevitably come first on this itinerary, for every visitor to Northampton soon finds himself confronted with this

quite extraordinary building. It is, of course, not the original mediaeval church, apart from the tower, and even that was rebuilt about forty years ago. It is a product of the wholesale rebuilding of Northampton which took place after the Great Fire of 1675 which destroyed most of the mediaeval city in a few hours. This explains its Christopher Wren-ish look, though the architect seems to have been Henry Bell who also designed the beautiful Customs House at King's Lynn, and the date of the rebuilding was circa 1680.

All Saints' is quite unique in appearance. It has a Gothic tower, fronted by a magnificent classical portico from around 1700 and surmounted by a charming Baroque cupola, with a large lanterned dome behind, the building being largely in the beautiful golden ironstone which is such a delightful feature of so many Northamptonshire buildings.

In theory this quaint jumble of Gothic and Classical should prove bewildering, but in fact the result is a work of tremendous character, absolutely individual and unforgettable. The interior is less rewarding, but it contains some fine woodwork, an interesting Narthex (where refreshments can be obtained) and four massive columns that help to support the dome.

Five minutes' walk to the north (up the Drapery and along Sheep Street) leads to what is undoubtedly Northampton's most famous and unusual church, the Church of the Holy Sepulchre; often called St. Sepulchre's and even locally known as "St. Seps". This is one of the very few remaining Round Churches in England, built by the Normans in imitation of the Holy Sepulchre in Jerusalem, and it is certainly the finest of all the extant specimens. The splendid circular nave, with its colossal columns and interesting wooden roof, is one of Northampton's major architectural treasures, and the whole church is a fascinating example of mediaeval craftsmanship, brilliantly extended in 1864 by Sir Gilbert Scott to include an apsidal chancel and side chapels, one of which contains a lovely window by the distinguished Victorian stained glass artist, Kempe.

The stately tower and spire complete a beautiful ensemble, again in the local golden ironstone, and the church is set in a well-timbered old churchyard, remarkably extensive for a town-centre situation.

A short walk down Bridge Street to the south of All Saints' lies another mediaeval church, St. John's, now a Roman Catholic church. Northampton has a Roman Catholic Cathedral and is the episcopal city of the largest Catholic diocese in England. St. John's is the only remaining part of the mediaeval Hospital of St. John, and, though small, is well worth a visit as it has been very skilfully reconstructed and adapted for Roman Catholic uses. It is yet another example of golden ironstone and recent demolitions nearby have opened up a good view of it as you approach from the Bridge Street side.

To the east of All Saints', again within about five minutes walk, is St. Giles', set in Northampton's most charming churchyard which in Spring is particularly beautiful with its many finely matured red and white chestnut trees. The noble ironstone tower has been tastefully repaired and the clock,

Top left: Capital in St Peter's Northampton
Right: St Peter's Northampton

which has a pretty black and gold dial, has a very melodious chime.

There are several interesting things to see inside, including a curious seventeenth century Justice's Chair and a mediaeval tomb; amateurs of Victoriana should not miss the great east window, a very fine example of Victorian glass painting, colourful and well-designed.

The western Norman doorway is a nineteenth century reconstruction, but the work was correctly done and it gives a good idea of what must once have been a superb piece of Norman masonry.

Last, but certainly not least, comes the magnificent Norman Church of St. Peter, which lies to the west of All Saints', again only five minutes walk away, this time down Gold Street and Marefair, just before you reach Northampton Railway Station. Until very recently this station was always known as the Castle Station, for it stands on the site of the great mediaeval castle which was originally the administrative centre of old Northampton. Several mediaeval parliaments were held within its walls; it was a favourite royal residence, especially of King John who seems to have had a special affection for Northampton, and it witnessed one of the most famous trials of mediaeval times, the arraignment of St. Thomas a Becket by Henry II in 1164. This forms one of the most powerful scenes in Tennyson's poetic drama "Becket".

The proximity of St. Peter's to the royal castle no doubt explains the remarkably rich Norman carving of the capitals of the columns in the interior, which Sir Nikolaus Pevsner has described as "startlingly lavish". They are of astonishing variety and individual freshness, and the great western arch beneath the tower is a tour de force of Norman inventiveness and professional skill.

The exterior of the tower has had to be recently restored and now presents an inevitably new appearance, but the inside remains virtually unaltered and should certainly not be missed on any visit to Northampton, however short. A superb Norman sepulchral carved stone slab has been preserved in the south aisle which is one of the most interesting individual treasures of the church.

All Saints' Northampton

Right: Holy Sepulchre Church Northampton

Towcester's Baroque Organ

Towcester, a perfect setting for Mrs. Gaskell's "Cranford", has a specially charming town centre which one can only hope will long be safely preserved from spoliation. The colouring of it alone is a delight – the rich deep golden ironstone of "The Saracen's Head", the red-tiled, flowerdecked and dormer-windowed front of "The Brave Old Oak", the quiet Georgian houses and the pretty spirelet of the little Town Hall, make up a very beautiful urban vista.

Even the Police Station is attractive! Built in the 1930's, before modern architectural barbrism reared its head, it is a picturesque Tudor college-style building running along the Watling Street which is now, thanks to the competition of the M.1. rather more peaceful than it used to be.

Towcester, small as it is, is full of interest, with memories of Mr. Pickwick at "The Saracen's Head" and a pleasant old cafe that commemorates his name. Antique shops are varied and surprisingly good and there is often fine marquetry furniture worth watching for. Other things worth looking at are the splendid late classical Gate Screen at the Racecourse entrance and the medieval Chantry House founded by Archdeacon Sponne in 1447. It has the date 1448 over the door.

Besides all this, lovers of Victoriana ought to pay a visit to the old Workhouse off the Brackley Road! It is a dignified golden stone classical building by the most famous of Victorian architects, Sir Gilbert Scott, whose work one so constantly encounters all over England as well as in Northamptonshire itself.

But perhaps the finest thing in Towcester is the superb late Baroque organ in the Parish Church, a truly remarkable possession.

It had nothing to do with Towcester originally. It was purchased at the great sale of the fantastic collection of William Beckford, the strange literary millionaire who built himself a wild Gothic palace at Fonthill Abbey with a monstrous and dizzy tower that finally crashed in ruins some years after it was built. Beckford left the world one lurid masterpiece of fiction, the macabre oriental fantasy "Vathek", which is generally recognised as a literary cornerstone of the Gothic Revival in English Literature.

He was equally famous for his collection of curios and among them the richly elaborate organ at Towcester was an outstanding specimen. It was actually a present to Towcester Church from Lord Pomfret who had acquired it at the Fonthill sale in 1817. It was thoroughly restored and rebuilt in 1967. This sumptuous, gay and splendid instrument, so strange to encounter in the solemn mediaeval setting of Towcester Church, is of French or Belgian make, though it belongs in spirit to some glittering golden Austrian rococo chapel.

Northamptonshire is not specially rich in historical musical instruments, though there are other fine organ cases at Stanford and Finedon, and an exquisite Edwardian design by Comper at St. Mary's, Wellingborough. Christ Church at Northampton, too, was recently the fortunate recipient of a splendid example, also Baroque in style, from the home of the Barratt family, St. David's at Kingsthorpe.

But the Towcester organ is easily the most precious of them all, and with its

Town Centre, Towcester

literary associations and its superb craftsmanship it must always be accounted a Northamptonshire Treasure indeed.

There are other things in Towcester Church well worth seeing, such as the curious tomb of Archdeacon Sponne. And the church is also celebrated for something that has left no visible memorial; one of the mediaeval priests who held the living of Towcester was Benedetto Gaetani who afterwards became one of the famous Popes of history as Boniface the Eighth. He was attacked by Dante in the "Divine Comedy" for his conduct of the Papacy, but he obviously had outstanding qualities, and among other things to his credit was his patronage of the great Florentine artist, Giotto.

He was Pope at the time of the building of the Queen Eleanor Crosses, though his relationship with her husband, Edward the First, was far from harmonious.

Entrance to Towcester Racecourse

This essay was written when Northampton still had a far greater variety of taverns than it now has, for many of the street corner pubs and smaller inns have disappeared in the general march of "progress".

However, I have decided to let the essay stand in its original form; I hope it may evoke pleasant memories among the many readers who will remember with affection some of the vanished hostelries here mentioned. *The King's Head* and even the Midland Red bus queues on the Mayorhold, *The Green Dragon, The Admiral Rodney, The Spread Eagle, The Peacock,* and several others are now no more, but fortunately some of the larger and more splendid buildings, like the *Abington Park Hotel* and *The Cock* at Kingsthorpe, are enjoying a vigorous reflorescence.

The *Abington Park Hotel,* for instance, has been lavishly re-Victorianised inside, complete with red plush banquettes, chandeliers, stuffed birds and Heaven knows what else, and *The Cock* has been so elaborately transmogrified that even its own architect wouldn't know it any more. But the exteriors of both these hotels have hardly been altered at all, and they remain as fine examples of the grander type of Victorian tavern architecture.

Taverns of Northampton

The Fire of 1675 destroyed most of the ancient hostelries of Northampton, and the effects of time have completed the work of the blaze. But here and there throughout the town a tavern survives, in a modern form, which can still trace its ancestry back for several centuries. *The Green Dragon* on the Mayorhold, for instance, has a very respectable history stretching at least as far as the Elizabethan era. The

Right: Two details of the Abington Park Hotel

present *Bantam Cock* on Abington Square reincarnates another inn with a long and interesting pedigree. It was the last house of the town before the development of Kettering Road.

Yet we have to admit that, to the outward eye, little enough remains of our hostelric past. We have, for instance, nothing to show in Northampton comparable with that exquisite and ancient timbered tavern *The Golden Lion* at Wellingborough, though the courtyard of *The Peacock* on the Market Square still maintains its quiet and dignified atmosphere of mail-coaches and Pickwickian prosperity.

But, as a reward for patient prowlings, some interesting things occasionally come to light. At *The Pomfret Arms* in Bridge Street, for example, there is now proudly and very artistically displayed an extraordinary grotesque stone head which was discovered during the rebuilding of the house. It belonged to St. Leonard's Hospital which stood on the site during the Middle Ages. The carving shows a high degree of skill in the mediaeval gargoyle tradition, and once seen its features are unforgettable.

Another interesting link with the past is *The King's Head,* a well built house with its dormer windows and charming proportions, looking out where the Midland Red bus queues congregate on the Mayorhold, formerly the municipal heart of ancient Northampton. And *The Old Black Lion,* rambling back almost to St. Peter's tower, is another agreeable old building on historic ground. It is closely linked with the Castle, which is the setting of so much of Shakespeare's "King John" and over whose melancholy ruins the London and North Western Railway finally and ruthlessly rode.

And, as if to compensate for what we lost, the modern taverns of the town are astonishingly plentiful! Many of these have fascinating links, at least in spirit, with earlier times. For example, it is a pleasantly stimulating imaginative exercise to sit in the lounge of *The Swan* and recreate in it the figure of Sir Henry Irving the actor, who visited it frequently when playing at the old Opera House at the end of last century.

And in the bars of *The Shakespeare* in Marefair, on the site of one of Northamptons' earliest theatres, the ghosts of Kean, Macready and other great actors of the nineteenth century hover in the air for those possessed of psychic powers and sufficient liquor.

A connection with the gipsy life of bygone days is kept up by the attractive coloured caravan blazoned on the signboard of *The Romany* in what used to be Gipsy Lane; once as much haunted by the Romany people as is that almost legendary green lane over Hunsbury Hill today. Mention of signboards reminds one that the most famous specimen of the whole district was the original, attributed to Hogarth, depicting the World's End at Ecton. It has long since vanished.

Several of the old village taverns are now well within the town limits. A beautiful and quite unspoilt example is *The Wheatsheaf* at Dallington, but perhaps of all our former village inns the *Cock Hotel* at Kingsthorpe is the finest. It is not, of course, in its present form the original building. A picture of this can be seen at Abington Museum, serene and tree-fringed, the very incarnation of the romantic dream of the rustic inn. But as it now stands it makes, with its neighbouring houses, a fine composition; especially in summer, framed against the rich foliage of Kingsthorpe Park. It has the air of a Cotswold Manor House or even of a corner of Oxford, and the treatment of the gables, roof and windows is especially happy. It must rank, indeed, as one of the town's best buildings.

Another excellent architectural composition is the *Abington Park Hotel.* Designed in the style of the French Renaissance, in attractively tinted red brick with silver-grey stone dressings, it has some fine carving, splendidly built chimneys, and a delightful porch with a fine ironwork projecting

Facade, Abington Park Hotel

lamp, which has been carefully preserved since the inn was finished in 1898.

Many other taverns of the town have their special points of interest. There is that bold stone bird perched over the door of *The Spread Eagle* in the Wellingborough Road. It used to glitter in the sun in the days when it was freshly gilt. There is the *Spinney Hill Hotel,* which, so I believe, shares with the *Sunnyside* the distinction of being the highest inn between here and the Ural Mountains in Russia! There is the delightful old cottage-style front of *The Squirrels* at Duston, looking as if it were

absolutely untouched since the seventeenth century. There is the charming little hanging wall-garden so surprisingly concealed behind *The Princess Royal,* which is a mass of colour in the summer months.

Then *The Admiral Rodney* boasts some excellently turned woodwork on the staircase handrails and posts, and indeed the general quality of the woodwork throughout is of a high standard.

Franklin's Hotel, a well built modern house, stands on the site of the old. It evokes memories of the days when peacocks and fireworks attracted thousands of people to the then famous Franklin's Gardens. Incidentally, the residents of St. James's End are fortunate to possess, all in a lump, a Hotel, a Rugby Football Ground and Tennis Courts together with the town's best Dance Hall.

Other houses have their special internal attractions. The new *Sunnyside* on Boughton Green Road has cleverly preserved the atmosphere of a comfortable private house, with its former billiard room converted into a most colourfully curtained lounge. *The Ram* in Sheep Street has a large and handsome lounge, with wall-lights and ceiling lights in profusion and a general air of pleasant warmth and cheerfulness.

But there is no end to the special features of Northampton's taverns. *The Plough,* for instance, which on market days becomes a bucolic metropolis in its own right, is peopled with the vigorous and varied influx of countrymen who give Northamptonshire its special and, let us hope, indestructible character.

The inns with peculiar names – *The Marquis of Carabas, The Old House at Home, The Swan and Helmet,* together with that now vanished curiosity of nomenclature *The Case is Altered* – have each their individuality, and usually their special clientele. And in a world which tends towards uniformity of thought and appearance, we can do with as much individuality in our daily lives as we can possibly preserve.

Left: Shakespeare Hotel
Below: Plough Hotel

Queen Eleanor's Cross

It was a winter's morning. Glittering in the frosty sunlight, an ancient silver-grey finger pointing up into the cold blue sky, the Queen's Cross stood calm and unshaken by the traffic of the London Road. From the exquisitely sculptured niches the time-battered figures of Queen Eleanor looked out, mysteriously enigmatic as the Gioconda smiling for ever on the passers-by in the Louvre.

Those fine statues, though now much crumbled, must in their springtime have been works of the first order of artistic excellence. The whole Cross, indeed, designed by John de Bello, is, like its compeers at Geddington and Waltham, a specimen of Gothic art at the height of its powers.

We are fortunate to possess within the confines of Northamptonshire two of the remaining three of the chain of Eleanor Crosses which originally adorned the route from Harby in Nottinghamshire where, in 1290, the Queen died, to Westminster where she was laid to rest.

Daughter of Ferdinand III of Castile and Joanna, Countess of Ponthieu, little is known of this merciful and benevolent Queen, except that she was universally beloved and a kindly and restraining influence on her lord, Edward the First, the "English Justinian", as he came to be styled from his many legal reforms.

But to this day her memory is kept green by these three wonderful memorial crosses, and, of course, in London a copy has been set up at Charing Cross, outside the station, on the site of the original monument.

Queen Eleanor's Cross, Hardingstone, begun 1291

As I took a last look at the figures of the Queen, the clouds finally cleared right out of the sky and, turning away into Delapre Park and on into Hardingstone, I saw the town spread out beneath me "bright and glittering in the smokeless air".

There it lay, factories, chimneys, steeples, cupolas, towers, streets, houses, hotels, cinemas, chapels, gardens, parks. On the northern horizon the distant long white block of the Fire Station. Closer to the foreground the just-discernible red bricks of the Opera House stage wall and the ventilator on its roof. In its earliest years the old theatre had a painted drop-curtain, in that delicious Victorian framed-picture convention, representing Queen Eleanor's Cross itself, though what happened to it, I could never learn. Far out to the east, the ancient slopes of Clifford Hill, which must surely have been a kind of beacon-tower for the primitive tribes who made it, flashing its fiery messages of danger across to the Hunsbury encampment and thence possibly to Borough Hill at Daventry and Arbury Hill at Badby.

Below, in the park itself, lay Delapre Abbey, its religious life long since swallowed up by time and its community of nuns for ever scattered. It was an interesting house in its day, being notable as the only convent of Cluniac Nuns ever established in England. It appears that its history was not always as tranquil as in the days of Margery de Wollaston, who was Abbess when Queen Eleanor's funeral cortege came to its gates. For instance the reign of her successor, Margery de Breke (1297–1319) was more troubled. In 1300 three nuns escaped and returned to secular life, whereupon a mandate from the Bishop to the Archdeacon of Northampton ordered him to denounce, with bell, book and candle, and in every church of the archdeaconry, Isabella Clouvil, Matilda de Thychemers (could this be Titchmarsh?) and Ermentrude de Newark.

Subsequent irregularities in the administration of the convent led to the excommunication of the Abbess Margery, who resigned in 1319.

It was in these meadows too that, in 1460, the army of Henry the Sixth was defeated at the Battle of Northampton, and the Yorkist faction established itself firmly in power.

Rising up behind the Abbey loomed the Gog and Magog of the Electric Light Works Cooling Towers, and I thought that if any of the primitive tribesmen of Hunsbury Hill returned to these slopes they would at once fall down and worship these monsters as twin-deities, guardians of the river-valley below. Certainly they would understand nothing else of the scene before them, except the eternal and time-defying streams of the Nene, for in their day dense forests covered Northampton, and over the site of the Market Square and up Abington Street and every other street the silence of the impenetrable forest was broken only by the howl of wolves.

Looking out again, I could trace Becket's Park with its (alas, now closed up!) Well. Historians may point out that St. Thomas a Becket must have left, when escaping from Northampton after his trial at the Castle, by the North Gate and not by Dern Gate. But the tradition of the Well dies hard, and the tale goes that the Saint lay concealed in the woodlands of Northamptonshire to baffle his pursuers.

A lady recently told me an amazing story of this. She met a gipsy at Becket's Well (before it was stopped up) filling a bottle with the water, and she asked him what he was doing. He had come, he said, all the way from Rockingham Forest to get water from this Spring which was famous among the Forest gipsies for its curative properties, especially for troubles of the eyes. And, besides, it was Becket's own Well. My friend asked him if he knew who St. Thomas a Becket was. "Oh yes", said the gipsy, "we hid him". If the poor gipsies make their pilgrimage now they will find the Spring stopped up, a blank stone slab in its place, and all their labour lost. Apparently the authorities thought the water was polluted. The gipsies of Rockingham Forest, however, had for eight hundred years thought very differently.

By this time I was getting hungry. But still the panorama below fascinated me constantly with its stream of daylight ghosts. And just out of sight, as I knew, lay others equally interesting. Shakespeare's grand-daughter, for instance, buried at Abington Church, James Hervey, that melancholy eighteenth century best-seller with his "Meditations Among the Tombs", born at Hardingstone itself and Rector of Weston Favell where he wrote and died.

And, of course, once my circle had started to expand in this way there was no stopping it. Out to the west, close to where the ever-visible tower and chimney of Berry Wood mark the skyline, lay Upton, venerable as the ancestral home of James Harrington, author of the celebrated "Oceana". In the great line of books depicting the Ideal Commonwealth, the line which includes More's "Utopia" and Bacon's "New Atlantis", "Oceana", though not much read today, was in its time a distinguished contribution to seventeenth century political philosophy, and in Northampton we ought to know it better.

But by this time Hunger had really conquered History and a green bus appeared in Hardingstone Lane. I got on it, was borne rapidly back past Queen's Cross again, and fifteen minutes later was eating my lunch in the forest of shops, streets, houses, etc., which, fifteen minutes earlier, was the subject of so much dreamy speculation.

Left: Delapre Abbey
Below: Cooling Towers

Pavilions at Stoke Park by Inigo Jones (copyright Country Life)

The Famous Pavilions at Stoke Bruerne

The Classical Renaissance in architecture reached England comparatively late, and Northamptonshire did not construct many really outstanding examples of it. The reason is that our county was already splendidly provided with both fine medieval churches and fine medieval manor houses which were largely adequate for all the ordinary needs of contemporary society.

But gradually a change came over architectural fashions, especially in domestic building, and in the 17th century it was many a nobleman's ambition to live in a house with a classical flavour to it instead of the picturesque but often uncomfortable old homes that had been good enough for his ancestors.

It was not unlike the fashion today for "modern" houses as opposed to the older type of house left over from the 19th century. Besides, European travel was becoming easier, especially for the wealthy, and many rich men went on tours of Italy and France where they would see beautiful examples of the fashionable classical style adapted to new palaces and chateaux. They would then come back to England fired with the desire to live in that sort of state themselves.

The most famous name in English architecture in the propagation of the new classical fashion was Inigo Jones, but very little of his absolutely authenticated work survives to support his enormous reputation. In Northamptonshire the Pavilions at Stoke Bruerne, the only survivors of a much larger house which was burnt down in the Victorian age, have, however, been attributed to him with considerable confidence. Another work which may very probably be his is the lovely classical Screen on the front of Castle Ashby which links together the east and west sides of the courtyard.

The Pavilions at Stoke Park are certainly very fine examples of the style of Jones, whether they are actually his or not, though it seems that the main part of the house (the part destroyed by fire) was built in a rather different manner.

Jones, born in 1573, came to maturity in the reigns of James the First and Charles the First, and he developed into the acknowledged chief figure of theatrical scene-designing of his day. He was the scenic master of the revels for many of the wonderful Court Masques which made the Jacobean and Caroline theatre so brilliant in stage history. And from a love of painting buildings in theatrical designs he graduated into being a genuine architect. He came strongly under the influence of the great Italian master, Palladio, whose example is obvious in famous buildings like the Queen's Villa at Greenwich and the Banqueting House in Whitehall, both by Jones.

It was Sir Francis Crane who built the 17th century house at Stoke Bruerne, and Bridges, the 18th century county historian of Northamptonshire, says that he brought the preliminary design back with him from Italy, and that Jones worked on it with him in carrying it out.

The plan of the house was that of a central block with wings connecting it to end-pavilions, and it is these pavilions which have survived and give a tantalising glimpse of what the whole great mansion must have been.

They have the much-loved Jonesian motif of giant pilasters down the sides, in this case of the Ionic kind – a feature which had been used by Michelangelo and Palladio in Italy, and also later on in France and Holland.

The importance of Stoke Park in architectural history is that it was the first house in England to be built on the Palladian plan of a central nucleus with pavilions extending out from it by colonnades. Its date was 1629–35, and Sir Francis Crane, who was head of the famous Mortlake Tapestry Works, only lived in it for a short time after its completion, though he had the honour of entertaining Charles the First at Stoke in the very year in which the great house was finished.

What we see today, therefore, is only a fragment of the original, but it is a very precious fragment and one which time has so far mercifully spared from spoliation and destruction.

Sessions House, Northampton, Details of Ceiling

The Devil in the Ceiling

The recent restoration of the dome of All Saints' Church at Northampton threw into relief the whole ensemble of the George Row scene, a view which has always charmed and delighted visitors.

Sir Nikolaus Pevsner, for instance, in his book on Northamptonshire, commented on the excellent picture that All Saints' makes against the Sessions House of the County Hall, with its Palladian extension to the west.

And it is probably no coincidence that the two buildings blend so admirably since the same architect, Henry Bell, of King's Lynn, almost certainly had a hand in both. The exact extent of his contribution has been much questioned, and in any case the original idea for the Sessions House seems to have come from an amateur, Sir Roger Norwich, who was M.P. for Northampton at the time of its projection. But Bell was the "professional" who apparently worked on the reconstruction of All Saints' after the Great Fire of Northampton in 1675, and he was probably also called in to supervise the translation of Sir Roger Norwich's ideas into definite form when the Sessions House came to be built.

Whoever deserves the credit, it is certainly a beautiful design. And it once seems to have looked even better since it had a pretty cupola on the roof, as can still be seen in some of the older prints. The date of the building, unlike the name of the architect, is definite enough, 1676–8.

Also certain is the name of the craftsman who produced the superb plaster ceilings of the main Court Rooms. This was the celebrated Edward Goudge who added this magnificent adornment between 1684 and 1688. He was as fine an artist in plaster as the famous Grinling Gibbons was in wood, and his work at Cambridge (and also what he probably did at Burghley House) is well enough known. Not nearly enough people, however, know of this masterpiece of his in our own town centre. The splendid central wreath of the rear court ceiling, with its wonderful plaster flowers, is a triumph of both technical and artistic achievement.

Also included in the decoration is a remarkable figure of a devil which is reputed to wag his tongue when witnesses are telling a lie, and in the front court there is a group of royal full-length portraits in fine gilt frames.

Until a few years ago the exterior was a lovely sooty-silver colour, the product of a couple of centuries of climatic exposure. But it was then decided to clean all the stonework and a somewhat curious pinky-yellow texture emerged. This is now in its turn toning down again and the beautiful frontage is once more harmonising nicely with the rich golden-brown of All Saints'. The design is slightly French in character, with a hipped roof, but fundamentally classical, having three extremely grand arched doors, though those on the front are never apparently put to any use.

Eight semi-circular Corinthian columns on the front and four flat-sided pilasters on the west give further dignity to the design, all these columns being of the "engaged" type, that is, set into the wall and not standing free.

Behind the Sessions House is one of Northampton's surprises, a calm green-lawned quadrangle with a wonderful view of the gables and towers of the Town Hall skyline.

In the adjoining County Hall offices there is a delightful small circular vestibule to the Council Chamber, also with a decorated plaster ceiling in the form of a dome, and elegant wooden columns and panelling. This was clearly of a much later date than the exterior, but harmonises with it well.

The whole ensemble of the buildings, with the dignified Georgian-style Judge's Lodgings adjoining the Sessions House and the Ionic-columned facade of the offices on the right, forms an essential part of the Northampton town centre scene; with the Gothic Town Hall nearby and the Lutyens War Memorial in All Saints' churchyard it makes a valuable contribution to the picture and one which should always be carefully preserved.

In fact, as far as anything connected with so awe-inspiring a place as a County Court can be called delightful, this Sessions House certainly is, though probably few who find themselves compelled to attend in it are in much of a mood to appreciate its beauties.

Perhaps the most famous case in its annals was the Rouse murder trial in the 1930's, a classic in criminal history, and made specially lurid by its incident of the blazing car (it is indeed usually known as "The Blazing Car Murder"). A tragic memento of it all is to be seen in the romantically overgrown churchyard of Hardingstone, where the crime was committed; a simple wooden cross was erected and still stands over a grave bearing the inscription "To The Memory Of An Unknown Man".

The Devil in the Ceiling

The Heaven Room in Burghley House

The Heaven Room at Burghley House has often been called the finest painted room in England. It is certainly a great tour-de-force of theatrical splendour, a piece of baroque magnificence more like a salon in a European Grand Duke's palace than a Northamptonshire nobleman's home.

Against a sumptuous background of Corinthian columns and classical friezes, an animated mass of half-naked mythological figures populates the scene. Cupids tumble upside-down out of heaven, flying creatures sail across the sky, faces peer from behind columns, and vast muscular men work at the forge of Cyclops depicted at one end of this astonishing apartment.

The painting covers the entire ceiling and walls, right down to the floor, and it is set off by a choice and finely coloured carpet. Completed in 1694, it measures 39 feet by 27 feet, is 24 feet high, and is the generally accepted masterpiece of the Italian artist Verrio who worked at Burghley for some twelve years in all. Not all tastes find themselves in sympathy with Verrio's riotous grand-opera style of decoration or with his exuberant but somewhat coarse sense of magnificence. But stunning his work undoubtedly is, and the brilliance of the colours, the luscious figures and the gaily garlanded columns make it all an enchantment for those who like to be overwhelmed by grandeur.

An interesting detail is that Verrio painted himself, looking oddly bald without his periwig, in a corner of the Cyclops' forge scene.

Queen Victoria used this apartment as a breakfast room on her visit in 1844. The thought of the demure young queen taking her morning meal against all those mighty unclad men is a theme for interesting contemplation!

Verrio, of course, painted other rooms at Burghley, but nothing else that overflowed all over the walls like this. The nearest in style is perhaps the ceiling of the Great Drawing Room where another general riot of classical figures, scantily attired, surrounds a shocked-looking peacock, apparently unable to believe his eyes at such a sight, and no wonder.

Yet another richly theatrical work by Verrio is the ceiling of the State Bedroom, more than ever like the ceiling of an opera house as it is circular in design. The theatrical effect is heightened by groups of figures breaking into the framework of the painting, recalling some of those excited and gesticulating groups of Italian and Austrian churches.

One of Verrio's designs for the Burghley decorative scheme is now in Northampton Central Art Gallery, an acquisition which the town was very fortunate to make a few years ago. It should not be judged as a painting in its own right, but as a model for something not intended to be viewed at close quarters.

Verrio seems to have had a royal time at Burghley for he was treated almost like a prince. His salary was £1,500 a year, a very large sum in the 17th century, and he had his own suite of apartments and special servant. Even his diet was carefully considered, and supplies of Italian liver sausage were sent over to him so that he should not feel homesick for sunny Italy among the damp meadows of Northamptonshire.

Burghley is the ancestral home of the Marquess of Exeter and is situated just outside Stamford. It is the most famous surviving example of an Elizabethan mansion and contains many more treasures beside the Verrio paintings. There are fireplaces of solid silver, tapestried and satin bedchambers, a Chinese Orange Court, a wonderful Great Hall with a hammerbeam roof, and endless other marvels.

If you have never seen it make certain that during the coming summer you miss it no longer, for taken as a whole it is easily the finest of all Northamptonshire's County Treasures.

Ceiling of the Heaven Room, Burghley House

Heaven Room, Burghley House (copyright Country Life)

BRACKLEY. NORTHAMPTONSHIRE

The Charms of Brackley

One of Northamptonshire's most attractive small towns, Brackley makes a very welcome half-way stopping place on the road from Northampton to Oxford. After the long and leafy lanes from Towcester it comes at last into sight about twenty miles out on the Oxford journey, and it always seems a kind of aperitif to the splendours of the great university city ahead. Right at the extreme tip of the county, it almost touches Oxfordshire, and with its fine Tudor-style schools and graceful high street it even seems like an Oxford in miniature. Magdalen College School in Brackley has strong ties with Oxford, and the great William of Waynflete, founder of Oxford's Magdalen College, took a close interest in the development of the school. The town was also a place of refuge from Oxford in time of plague.

Nothing in Brackley is visually outstanding, but the buildings blend into a quiet and so far almost unspoilt ensemble. All lovers of the old Great Central Railway were deeply sorry to see the closing of that fine broad line which, of course, ran through Brackley, and the only melancholy remains of it there are the still standing red brick station buildings. But, this apart, Brackley is much as it always was, and it has a specially lovely relic of the eighteenth century in its Town Hall, a serene and compact small gem, attractively placed on an island site in the main street, and with a pretty cupola surmounting it. Built by the first Duke of Bridgewater in 1706, it dominates the Brackley townscape in an unforgettable way.

There are many good Georgian houses also, the best perhaps being the Crown Hotel, which is reputed to have a history going back at least to the reign of King John, though it is now almost entirely Georgian in structure. Its finely proportioned windows, including a Venetian centre-piece, are an inviting foretaste of the warmth and curtained cosiness inside, and on a winter's day it provides a welcome break on the Northampton to Oxford journey.

I have found Brackley an interesting place for antiques, and a lot of richly decorated porcelain vases and plates often find their way here. The little town, like Towcester, so suggestive of the atmosphere of Mrs. Gaskell's "Cranford", is a perfect setting for antique hunting, set as it is in the middle of miles of rich greenery, remnants of ancient forests and lush golden-flowered meadowland. It has known stirring events too, for in the days of Magna Carta the Barons gathered at Brackley, and their preliminary demands to King John there were a prelude to the decisive meeting at Runnymede when John was finally forced to yield to them.

Far too many people simply flash through Brackley without stopping; understandably, no doubt, if they are in a hurry to push on to either Oxford or Northampton. But its subtle charms are not to be gulped in by whizzing through its main street in a tearing haste. It is a leisurely little place, and it needs a leisurely inspection to do it justice.

It is becoming more and more difficult now to find small country towns that have successfully resisted the encroachments of supermarkets, the fringing by modern housing estates and the grotesqueries of the gaunt sodium lamp. But Brackley has done so very commendably to date, and it is to be hoped that it will go on being its own charming little self for many generations to come.

Brackley (copyright Aerofilms Ltd.)

Earls Barton - A Thousand Years of History

The year 1970 saw the celebration of the millenary of Earls Barton church, ten centuries of history massed behind that solid and world-renowned Saxon tower. Of all Northamptonshire's county treasures this is probably the best-known for if you open any text-book of English architecture one of the first illustrations is almost certain to be of Earls Barton tower. Proud in its massive Saxon grandeur, it is one of only a handful of monuments left from the dim centuries of King Alfred and Canute and the half-barbaric days before the Norman Conquest.

There seems little doubt that the tower itself stands on the site of a primitive fortress of the Ancient Britons, one of those mysterious hill-stations which kept watch against Scandinavian or Germanic invaders coming down the Nene in their war-boats and making for big tribal encampments like Hunsbury Hill. There was probably a whole line of those satellite camps at various points along the Nene Valley, ready to send fire or smoke signals back to the headquarters at Hunsbury whenever danger threatened from the east. Beacon Hill at Wollaston, Whiston hill, Earls Barton itself, and certainly Clifford Hill were part of the chain.

And still that grand but grim tower of Earls Barton suggests the fortress-like character of its origin. By the time it was built, however, England was developing a peace-time civilisation of its own, with its own poetry, beautiful metalwork, and jewellery like the lovely King Alfred's Jewel now in the Oxford Museum.

The grey old tower, with its battlements and clock as the only later additions, is even now a great landmark, for miles around. Its curious stone bands in X and diamond shapes and half-circles and strips are probably an echo of earlier timber styles of building. The little triangular windows and the "long and short work" at the corners of the tower are other typically Saxon motifs.

Apart from this there is little adornment at all. The whole tower is a stark contrast to its lovely neighbour across the valley, the exquisitely decorated Whiston, which seems to have been the last church built in England before the Reformation.

Along with Brixworth, also in Northamptonshire, Earls Barton is the most considerable of England's Saxon remains. And the church as a whole, taken as a piece of living history, is perhaps even more remarkable than Brixworth because it enshrines work of almost every century from the tenth to the twentieth. The tower dates from the tenth, the south doorway from the twelfth, the aisles from the thirteenth and the tower arch from the fourteenth century. There is a brass from the sixteenth century and a pulpit from the seventeenth. The south porch is from the nineteenth century and the Northampton artist Henry Bird's painted panels on the chancel screen link the fifteenth century and the twentieth.

1970, the year of celebration of Earls Barton's history, therefore, was not simply a thousandth milestone in the history of the ancient Saxon tower. It saw also the celebration of a thousand years of continuous development in addition to the church itself. A marvellous witness, in fact, to the staying power of Christianity through ten centuries of constant change in the pattern of human life.

The millenary was celebrated in the village with a six months programme, from April to November, entitled "Festival 1000", The events included "Son et Lumiere", a modern ballet, a pageant, "Noye's Fludde", a "Paint-in" weekend, a "mammoth carnival", "Everyman", a fireworks display, flower festivals, a horticultural show, a "Month of Dance", a poetry competition, and numerous exhibitions.

Fawsley

Much of my childhood was spent at Newnham where my great-aunt lived in the lovely old watermill on the banks of the infant Nene. How leafy and drowsy the lanes all seemed in those far-off pre-war days! How golden the wildflowers! How fragrant the blackcurrant jam, in its little silver dishes, which we always had for tea!

Fawsley Park was only a comfortable walk away and we had many an enchanting hot summer afternoon there by the ruined Dower House and the exquisitely curving lake. Even then the great House was

Above: Hall in Fawsley Park

empty and standing in melancholy grandeur, with its magnificent hall and the mysterious little embattled chamber above the oriel window where the famous Martin Marprelate tracts were printed on a secret printing press.

Recently I went over to Fawsley again and was delighted to see that the church, with its wonderful heritage of fine tombs and ancient stained glass, was still in very good condition in spite of its extreme loneliness and apparent lack of nearby houses and residents to support it. There is, however, always need of money to preserve these ancient fabrics, and certainly no local treasure could be worthier of assistance than this splendid old church.

It is really the ancestral chapel of the great Knightley family who were for so long the lords of Fawsley Manor. Fascinating in its isolation in superb parkland setting, it would be an ideal scene for one of Montague James's ghost stories. And though I have never seen it on a moonlit winter's night, I can imagine it gleaming in ghostly majesty as it looks out towards the distant Dower House which is itself, of course, equipped with a fully-authenticated ghostly horseman.

You enter through a charming little thirteenth century doorway, and are at once among a collection of family memorials almost unsurpassed in any Northamptonshire church. In the north aisle is a superb wall monument, vast, impressive, and now rich with gold and gleaming again in lavish colour, just as it must have been when first erected. This magnificent work, which extends along the north wall, is a monument to Knightleys of several generations and is elaborately detailed with classical cherubs and an enormous pediment.

Another fine work is the coloured alabaster altar-tomb memorial to Sir Richard Knightley, who died in 1534, and his wife. This exquisite example of sixteenth century carving has recumbent effigies of Sir Richard and his lady, gorgeously dressed, with small figures of their numerous family, eight sons and four daughters, most artistically disposed in panels at the sides of the tomb.

There are also some fine sepulchral brasses let into the floor of the church. One of these is a memorial to the distinguished Knightley who built the Hall.

The windows glow with ancient heraldic glass and Flemish medallions of very beautiful quality. They alone would make a visit to Fawsley Church well worth while.

At a time when so much of England is being ruined by miles of characterless housing it is deeply gratifying to be able to ride out just a few miles from Northampton and find oneself in this glorious unspoiled estate of Fawsley. Lonely, proud, splendid in its beauty, it still has its great trees intact and its marvellous vistas in every direction.

It is one of Northamptonshire's finest County Treasures and one which must be preserved at all costs. It must be handed down to the future as a most memorable example of what we have inherited from our country's richly storied past.

The Churches of Matthew Holding

St Matthew's, Holy Trinity, St Mary's, St Paul's and Christ Church.

The mediaeval churches of Northampton are justly renowned. Open almost any illustrated history of English architecture and you will find references to St Peter's, St John's or the Church of the Holy Sepulchre, along with their yet more famous county neighbours, Brixworth and Earls Barton. Brixworth has even been described as the most remarkable architectural monument of its period north of the Alps.

But I should like to say something about the modern churches of Northampton designed by the late Matthew Holding. I feel that it is time Holding's work received more notice, at all events by the citizens of the town for which he did so much.

As a group, his churches are far superior to anything else the nineteenth century church-builders left us in Northampton, though another excellent design was St Edmund's, opened in 1852, which was admired by one of the most distinguished of Victorian architects for the "honesty" of its composition. Holding was a pupil of the celebrated Pearson, the architect of Truro Cathedral and of St Augustine's,

St Matthew's Northampton, Interior

Kilburn, whose fine tower and spire you pass every time you go to London by rail. It is on the right, five minutes or so before the train gets in to Euston.

Like his great master, Holding was in revolt against the fussy heaviness of the Victorian "St Pancras Station" school of ecclesiastical Gothic, and all his churches show a remarkable purity of design.

St Matthew's is perhaps the best example of this, for there the surprising effect of richness is achieved with extremely little surface ornament. In fact, if you examine the exterior of St Matthew's carefully you will find no real decoration at all – the effect of richness is produced by the skilful cutting of the mouldings. There is virtually no conscious ornamentation.

Very graceful is the effect of the church as seen from the East End, especially in the early morning with the sun making a glittering fire of the windows in the apse and the Lady Chapel, and the lofty spire, with its golden weather vane, rising up behind. There is another fine view of the spire from the Spinney Hill area of Kettering Road, while from the road to Boughton Green the whole building dominates the landscape with truly cathedral-like grandeur. Other interesting features of the exterior are the fine lead fleche and the flying buttresses, and the entire ensemble is a beautiful essay in colour – brown stone, white spire, red roof, grey fleche, gold vane. Inside, one's attention is struck by the lightness of the whole design, and the iron screen adds notably to the sense of mystery which pervades the beautiful apse.

St Matthew's is undoubtedly Matthew Holding's masterpiece, but I would hesitate in deciding which of the other churches should rank second. As an exterior I would at once say Holy Trinity; as an interior, St Mary's, Far Cotton.

At Holy Trinity the fenestration, in Perpendicular style, is quite outstanding. Note the admirably deep cutting of the mouldings, the fine East and West windows, and the wonderful treatment of the clerestory. The pinnacles, too, are very good, and only the tower, despite being set in an original way over one of the transepts, is somewhat ineffective. In fact, the whole design would really show up to greater advantage without the tower at all. The interior lacks ecstasy, perhaps, though it is beautifully light and forms a delightful contrast to the rich golden brown exterior.

It is a pity that the church is so tucked away, off all main roads, so that it is far less known than it should be to visitors. The North elevation, for example, although extremely fine in design and execution, is almost completely invisible to the passer by.

St Mary's, of course, is of all Holding's interiors the most perfect. His interiors do not, perhaps, on the whole, match his exteriors, but St Mary's is an outstanding exception. The lovely roof and superb treatment of the apse with vaulting and stone ribbing suggests a mediaeval monastic chapel, dignified and yet intimate.

Holy Trinity, Northampton

St Matthew's, Northampton

The exterior is quite good, especially the spire as seen from a distance, and the detached campanile effect is interesting. The fenestration, as compared with Holy Trinity, however, is undistinguished, and everything else about the church pales beside the magnificent internal design.

St Paul's, Semilong, has, on the whole, a less individual character than the others of the group, but it has its very charming little bell tower and the double West windows are quite fine. Apart from these the fenestration again cannot match that at Holy Trinity.

About Christ Church it is difficult to speak fairly, for it is unfinished and so not really judgeable. From the picture hanging inside it appears that the great tower would have been superb and have made a fine eastern approach to the town, like St Matthew's spire. But, even so, the general composition is not entirely satisfactory, and the interior again fails to match the exterior. It is somewhat cold in effect, though the great transepts and organ-loft are good, and the massive East window, if a full scale reredos is ever placed below it, will form a splendid climax to the sanctuary. Otherwise the fenestration (and the pinnacle work) is again unequal to that of Holy Trinity. Matthew Holding himself only lived to see the completion of the nave and transepts, the chancel being added after the first World War.

The general quality of these five churches is extremely high in view of the fact that they were all built simply as nineteenth century suburban churches, i.e. none was for a specially distinguished position and only at St Matthew's was there a really good site. There are family resemblances in all five, all being in brown stone with silver-grey relief. Happily appropriate to the local building tradition, they carry on the style of the older churches of the town, yet in a manner unmistakably Matthew Holding's own.

The Northampton Repertory Theatre

The red and gold auditorium of the Northampton Repertory Theatre, formerly known to residents of the town as the Opera House and which some call the Royal Theatre, is now probably looking as lovely as at any time in its long history of 88 years.

It is a miniature masterpiece of Victorian theatre, designed by the most eminent of 19th century English theatre architects, C. J. Phipps. Phipps was to the 19th century theatre what Sir Gilbert Scott was to Victorian church building – the undisputed Maestro. He built forty theatres in Great Britain, including his masterpiece, Her Majesty's in London. Those with a knowledge of the difficulty of working in such a cramped site as that in Northampton will appreciate the manipulative dexterity of Phipps's scheme. A minor miracle was the grafting on of the Guildhall Road foyer and

Left: Repertory Theatre, Northampton, from the painting by T. Osborne Robinson

pit-staircase, cloakrooms, bar, manager's and other offices at right angles to the main building; while the ingenuity of the staircase leading to the stalls, via the circular passage behind the dress circle, borders on genius. Backstage other feats were performed, the culmination being the linking up of the stage, by means of a tunnel under Swan Street, with the paint room and dressing rooms on the other side of the road. It is a building which not only rambles and is not ashamed to ramble, but overcomes all obstacles in its rambling with complete abandon.

The theatre is still very much as it was in its early days. The dimly gilded proscenium and elegantly columned boxes, the iron columns supporting the circle-tier, the horseshoe rim of the dress circle and the neatly boxed little upper circle behind, together with the melange of corridors and unexpected flights of stairs leading apparently nowhere: this enchanting jumble remains just as our grandfathers knew it.

Its history falls into two clearly defined periods, 1884–1927 and 1927 to the present time. Before the erection of the New Theatre on Abington Street in 1912, it was the home of the principal touring companies, and they continued to visit it almost up to its acquisition by the Repertory Company at the end of 1926.

Before the Repertory Company took over in 1927, the stage, narrow but surprisingly deep and high, resounded for forty years with the full-blooded accents of old-style drama, Shakespeare, opera both Grand and Comic, "screaming farce", burlesque, pantomime and George Edwardes Musical Comedy. There were also occasional "stock" seasons of small travelling repertory companies – in fact, the whole gamut of the British Touring Theatre in the days of its splendour. Sir Henry Irving, Benson, and most of the great names of the late Victorian and Edwardian stage played here.

Not until 1927 did the theatre really become independent in the sense of maintaining its own permanent company. Since then it has gone on comfortably, housing well over a thousand plays and something like five million playgoers. What a dramatic banquet has been spread before Northampton since 1927 at the Repertory Theatre: Shakespeare, Ibsen, Shaw, Sheridan, Moliere, Wilde, Maugham, Synge, Pinero Chekhov and many lesser delights have been served, and nearly always well served for the palate of our fortunate town. For fortunate we are, theatrically speaking, and many a big city has not such a record of theatrical activity as we can point to from 1884 to the present time.

The theatre was redecorated a few years ago, and various handsome items of furnishing have since been added so that it is now one of the most charming interiors of its kind in England. Red and gold was kept as the predominant colour scheme, and the rich red brocade drop-curtain blends beautifully with the crimson plush seating, door curtains, red lamp shades and candelabras. There are other decorative touches, like the French clock on the mantelpiece in the foyer, the red and gold chairs, and the fine gilt chandelier in the booking hall.

The former drop-curtain, with a pretty Venetian scene surrounded by painted draperies, is fortunately still preserved at the theatre, though not normally in use any longer. It is a valuable relic of the now lost art of the Victorian pictorial Act Drop.

A recent minor disaster was the accident which destroyed the iron and coloured glass verandah fixed to the facade, but the inside of the building has survived in its full late Victorian splendour. Its history since the founding of the Northampton Repertory Company in 1927 was chronicled in 1948 by Aubrey Dyas in "Adventure in Repertory". It is to be hoped that some enthusiast will one day write the full story of its fascinating Victorian and Edwardian years from 1884 to 1926.

Castle Ashby

Of all the great parks of Northamptonshire that of Castle Ashby is probably the finest. But many visitors who enjoy the magnificent House, with its famous woodwork, its tapestries, its priceless paintings, and its exquisite china and furniture, tend to overlook some of the interesting things to be seen in the grounds.

Their grandest feature is the noble South Avenue of fine trees which goes down to the Bedford Road and continues on past it for a considerable distance. This is the avenue whose elaborate gates and grey stone gate-houses you pass on the left, between Denton and Yardley Hastings, as you go from Northampton to Bedford. They form one of the most beautiful entrances to any park in England, and are equal, if not superior, to any of the college entrances on the Backs at Cambridge.

This tremendous South Avenue is perhaps the nearest thing an English country park has to show to the great avenues of Versailles, and it makes an impressive approach to the Castle.

But close to the House there is also a great deal to see, both in buildings and ornamental features. On the west, the normal entrance side from the pretty stone-built village, there are the Jacobean Stables, and nearby is the curious Victorian "Water Tower" by Sir M. D. Wyatt. Curious it must be called rather than beautiful, and yet it has now become so much a part of the scene that it is difficult to imagine Castle Ashby without it. It dates from 1865 and is a typical piece of "country house Victoriana". Sir M. D. Wyatt also designed the intricate and rich terra cotta entrances to the south of the large lawn, though the exquisite iron gates themselves are apparently of Italian origin.

Terra cotta was also used for the balustrading of the terraces on the east and north sides of the surrounding gardens. They are famous for their inscriptions which are a parallel to the Latin lettering round the parapet of the House, though in this case they are in English and with different texts.

Another of Wyatt's works which should certainly not be missed is the splendid Orangery, just inside the enclosed part of the gardens south of Castle Ashby Church. This long and stately building in the Italian style is one of Wyatt's masterpieces, finely proportioned and with a frieze of figures above the central part. It is partnered by a handsome stone screen, "gloriette" is the technical name, at the other end of the Italian garden, which also dates from mid-Victorian days.

Northampton people will be specially interested in the curious walls of the kitchen garden further on, for they were designed by E. W. Godwin, the architect of Northampton Town Hall.

But of course the Victorians only completed at Castle Ashby what earlier ages had begun, and the general magnificence of the grounds was originally the work of Capability Brown, the prince of 18th century landscape gardeners, and indeed probably the finest landscape artist in western history. The charming little columned temple in the park, at some distance from the House, is a relic of the days of Brown, as are the Dairy and the Aviary.

Of the treasures of the Castle itself there is no need to say anything in commendation; their splendours are well enough known. But all visitors should make a point of seeing also the church close by, with its superb brass in the chancel to William Ermyn, a rector of Castle Ashby who died in 1401. This is specially notable for the details of the saints figured on the border of the cope. There are some good marble monuments in the church, and several interesting tombs in the churchyard by the entrance to Wyatt's Orangery.

The Castle, then, is not by any means the only thing to see on this wonderful estate. The treasures of the park are a feast in themselves.

Terracotta Balustrading at Castle Ashby "The grass withereth and the flower fadeth but the word of God endureth for ever"

Althorp-Home of the Spencers

Althorp House (copyright Aerofilms Ltd.)

The cool external appearance of Althorp House, home of the Spencer family for sixteen generations, conceals an interior of sumptuous splendour in which paintings, porcelain and furniture combine to form an ensemble of almost regal magnificence.

Very close to Northampton, Althorp lies just beyond the village of Harlestone. Its parish church is Great Brington which contains the superb array of Spencer family tombs from the sixteenth, seventeenth and eighteenth centuries.

Althorp has been an inhabited house for hundreds of years; the first Sir John Spencer bought the estate in 1508, and already there was a house there of considerable antiquity. Around 1573 this ancient manor was enlarged to make an open courtyard and some of the original structure was preserved, although little is to be seen of it in the present predominantly eighteenth century residence.

This was largely the work of Henry Holland, who entirely reconstructed the house and gave it its orderly classical lay-out completing it about 1790. A late seventeenth century engraving, however, by Kip, shows that the predecessor of the Holland house had a somewhat similar appearance, rather more French perhaps in design, with formal gardens that have been attributed to the great French garden artist, Le Nôtre. The diarist Evelyn visited this house in 1688 and described it as a palace, and certainly in the Kip engraving it resembles, like Boughton, a miniature Versailles or Schonbrunn although it was also described as "disposed after the Italian manner".

Holland's work was not merely an artistic reconstruction; it was structurally necessary as well, for the older house had begun to give indications of impending collapse. He produced, on the whole, a very satisfying design, veneering the basic material of light grey brick with "mathematical tiles" behind which are the bricks of the Elizabethan house, which in turn concealed the ancient stonework of the original mediaeval building.

Fundamentally what we see today, therefore, is Holland's design, though in the Victorian age some excellent additional work was done by Macvicar Anderson, who built the Dining Room in 1876–8. The house is surrounded by a great and noble park, with magnificently matured trees and, though a vast residence by modern standards, it has never been unmanageably huge or presented any insurmountable problems.

The real glories of Althorp are inside, and it has long been nationally and even internationally famous for its marvellous collection of paintings, one of the most splendid in England, its wonderful silver and ceramics and its fine French and other furniture. In 1970 the Victoria and Albert Museum published an illustrated booklet entitled "Treasures from Althorp", and this contains a good selection of pictures of the principal artistic masterpieces of the house. The Van Dycks are particularly fine and include a haunting "St. Matthew", while the seventeenth century portraits include a lovely Lely of Barbara Villiers, Duchess of Cleveland. A striking "Duchess of Marlborough" by Kneller admirably captures the tempestuous nature of the Sarah Jennings who was afterwards to make Vanbrugh's architectural career at Blenheim Palace such a bed of thorns.

The Reynolds portraits are also of the first order and very famous. His "Lavinia

Bingham, Viscountess Althorp" is one of the most exquisite portraits produced in the entire eighteenth century.

The silver at Althorp is of princely quality and includes the remarkable collection of Marlborough Plate. The pieces by Lamerie and Gilpin are outstanding, and there is a fine set of twelve lily candelabra of 1788 by William Pitts.

Lovers of porcelain will enjoy the very fine examples of Chelsea, Meissen, Sèvres, Chinese, Japanese and Italian work.

The furniture too is of the highest quality. Particularly interesting is the set of twenty six white and gold armchairs which came from the great ballroom at Spencer House in London and date from about 1764. Another very handsome set of chairs is the French "cabriole back stools", which were made in 1791 by François Hérve to an order by Holland himself.

Althorp was once also world-famous for the literary treasures which formed its great library, the richest private collection of books in Europe. They were, however, sold at the end of last century and now constitute a prominent section of the John Rylands Library in Manchester.

The Spencers have always been deeply devoted to Althorp and their great inheritance, transmitted to them through many generations, is displayed throughout this serene and beautiful house with great taste and sense of history.

County of Spires

Left: Spire of St Peter & St Paul Kettering
Below: St Michael's Bugbrooke

Just as Oxford is famous as the City of Dreaming Spires so Northamptonshire is known throughout the world as the County of Spires and Squires. But how far is it true? Are our churches predominantly crowned with spires and our countryside absolutely overflowing with squires?

As far as the squires are concerned the old saying has always been true enough and is still so today; comparatively few of the numerous country houses of Northamptonshire have been either demolished or turned into institutions and there are many "lords of the manor" still resident in the county.

But what about spires? Were they ever in fact as plentiful as towers on our churches? And even with the Victorian additions, such as St. Matthew's and St. Mary's, Far Cotton, in Northampton and the splendid Braunston Church near Daventry, are they as numerous as towers today?

The answer is quite definitely no, for fewer than half the churches of Northamptonshire have spires, though there is a particularly beautiful and extensive cluster of them down the Nene Valley which no doubt gave rise to the original saying.

But the Nene in its upper course, and right through the area around Northampton town, has very few spires to show, though there is a charmingly humble specimen at Newnham, near the source of the river, made specially interesting by the "open plan" of the arched space below. A few miles further down there are two more delightful though still quite small examples at Bugbrooke and Kislingbury. All three of these spires are beautifully backed by trees as you approach from a distance, and Bugbrooke is set in a specially lovely and tree-rich churchyard.

The town of Northampton itself, however, has still only four spires in all, even listing Kingsthorpe, which was formerly a quite separate village, as one of them. And if you look at most of those eighteenth century drawings of Northampton as seen from Hunsbury Hill, only Kingsthorpe and

St. Sepulchre's are visible, for the two spires by Matthew Holding, St. Matthew's and St. Mary's were not to adorn the skyline until the end of the nineteenth century.

Then as you leave the town and travel down the river valley it is some time before the Spire Country really begins. Great Houghton, of course, has a fine little eighteenth century spire, very originally set on a circle of small columns and designed by David and John Hiorne. It was David Hiorne who also built Daventry church with its somewhat similar obelisk spire.

But apart from this it is entirely towers for some distance along both sides of the valley – Little Houghton, Cogenhoe, Whiston, Billing, Ecton and the famous Saxon specimen at Earl's Barton. Not until Wilby, an enchantingly beautiful example rising up with a remarkable octagonal stage from the square base of the tower, does the "Spire Country" come into view. From then onwards, through Wellingborough and Wollaston and the exquisitely proportioned Easton Maudit, the stately procession starts.

And it is not only along the slopes of the valley that the spires appear; one of the finest in the county, for example, the magnificently soaring spire of Kettering, is several miles away, though it is a landmark for many miles around.

But it is the Nene Valley which is the real home of these lovely and graceful stone needles stabbing the horizon with, as it seems, ever-increasing beauty as you proceed eastwards towards Peterborough. Specially fine is the cluster of Rushden, Higham Ferrers and Raunds, all of absolutely first-class interest; less famous, but an excellent piece of design, is Irchester, and then further on there are the splendours of Oundle and the group that culminates in Warmington. The churches of this group were particularly admired by all the great Victorian architects from Sir Gilbert Scott himself downwards, and this explains why

so many of the hundreds of Victorian church spires scattered over England and Scotland have a familiar look to Northamptonshire people since many of them were in fact inspired by Nene Valley examples.

Even in Northamptonshire itself you can see a number of "Home Inspired" specimens too, such as the two Holding spires already mentioned, and that lonely, dramatic and extremely romantic tower and spire at Little Brington, all that is left of the church built by Hardwick in 1865 and which still rises, proud and solitary, and gleams in solemn grandeur if you catch a glimpse of it either against the setting sun or the rising moon.

Left to right:
St Peter & St Paul, Easton Maudit.
Holy Cross Daventry
St Mary's Great Houghton